Shire County Guide 36

WORCESTERSHIRE

Barry Freeman

D1070201

Shire Publications Ltd

Published in 1996 by Shire Publications Ltd, Cromwell House, Church Street, Princes Risborough, Buckinghamshire HP27 9AA, UK.
Copyright © 1996 by Barry Freeman. First published 1996. Shire County Guide 36. ISBN 0 7478 0311 0.
Barry Freeman is hereby identified as the author of this work in accordance with section 77 of the Copyright, Designs and Patents Act 1988.

Printed in Great Britain by CIT Printing Services, Press Buildings, Merlins Bridge, Haverfordwest, Dyfed SA61 1XF.

British Library Cataloguing in Publication Data. Freeman, Barry F. Worcestershire. – (Shire county guide; 36) 1. Worcestershire (England) – Guidebooks I. Title 914.2'44' 04859 ISBN 0-7478-0311-0.

Acknowledgements

Photographs are acknowledged as follows: Cadbury Lamb, pages 9, 10, 13, 16, 18, 23, 27, 30, 38, 42, 46, 52, 53 (lower), 58, 60, 61, 71, 74, 75 (both), 77, 80, 82, 83, 84, 90, 98, 99, 101; the Museum of Worcester Porcelain, page 93; the City of Worcester Museum, page 92. All other photographs by Kathleen Freeman. The maps were produced by Robert Dizon using Ordnance Survey material. The National Grid References in the text are included by permission of the Controller of Her Majesty's Stationary Office.

Ordnance Survey grid references

Although information on how to reach most of the places described in this book by car is given in the text, National Grid References are also included in many instances, particularly for the harder-to-find places in chapters 3, 4 and 8, for the benefit of those readers who have the Ordnance Survey 1:50,000 Landranger maps of the area. The references are stated as a Landranger sheet number followed by the 100 km National Grid square and the six-figure reference.

To locate a site by means of the grid references, proceed as in the following example: Kemerton Camp (OS 150: SO 957402). Take the OS Landranger map sheet 150 ('Worcester and the Malverns'). The grid numbers are printed in blue around the edges of the map. In more recently produced maps these numbers are repeated at 10 km intervals throughout the map, so that it is not necessary to open it out completely.) Read off these numbers from the left along the top edge of the map until you come to 95, denoting a vertical grid line, then estimate seven-tenths of the distance to vertical line 96 and envisage an imaginary vertical grid line 95.7 at this point. Next look at the grid numbers at one side of the map (either side will do) and read *upwards* until you find the horizontal grid line 40. Estimate two-tenths of the distance to the next horizontal line above (i.e. 41), and so envisage an imaginary horizontal line across the map at 40.2. Follow this imaginary line across the map until it crosses the imaginary vertical line 95.7. At the intersection of these two lines you will find Kemerton Camp.

The Ordnance Survey Landranger maps which cover Worcestershire are sheets 138, 139 and 150. Very small areas of the county are found on maps 149 and 151.

Cover: *The Malvern Hills towards Worcestershire Beacon. (Reproduced by courtesy of Malvern Hills District Council.)*

Contents

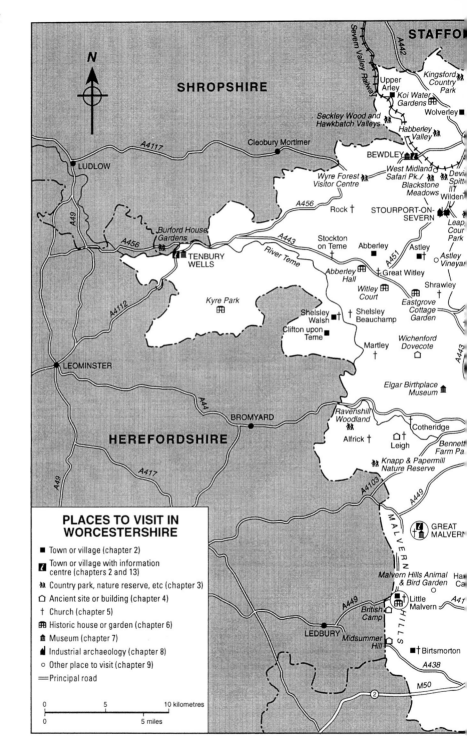

N

SHROPSHIRE

STAFFO[RD]

Severn Valley Railway

A442

Upper Arley ■
Koi Water Gardens ⊞

Kingsford 🐾 Country Park

Wolverley ■

Seckley Wood and Hawkbatch Valleys 🐾

Habberley Valley 🐾

A4117

Cleobury Mortimer ●

BEWDLEY

LUDLOW ●

Wyre Forest Visitor Centre 🐾

West Midland Safari Pk./ 🐾
Blackstone Meadows

Devi[l's]
Spitt[le]
II7
Wilden ■

A49

A456

Rock †

STOURPORT-ON-SEVERN

Leap[gate]
Cour[t]
Park

Burford House Gardens

A456

Stockton on Teme †

Abberley ■

Astley ■†

Astley Vineyar[d]

A443

River Teme

TENBURY WELLS

Abberley Hall ⊞

†Great Witley

A451

Shrawley †

Kyre Park ⊞

Witley Court ⊞

Eastgrove Cottage Garden ⊞

A4112

Shelsley Walsh ■†

†Shelsley Beauchamp

Clifton upon Teme ■

Wichenford Dovecote ⌂

LEOMINSTER ●

Martley †

A443

Elgar Birthplace Museum 🏛

A44

BROMYARD ●

Ravenshill Woodland 🐾

Cotheridge †

HEREFORDSHIRE

Alfrick †

Leigh ⌂†

Bennett[s] Farm Pa[rk]

A417

A49

Knapp & Papermill Nature Reserve 🐾

A4103

A449

MALVERN

GREAT MALVER[N] 🏛

PLACES TO VISIT IN WORCESTERSHIRE

■ Town or village (chapter 2)

🄳 Town or village with information centre (chapters 2 and 13)

🐾 Country park, nature reserve, etc (chapter 3)

⌂ Ancient site or building (chapter 4)

† Church (chapter 5)

⊞ Historic house or garden (chapter 6)

🏛 Museum (chapter 7)

◢ Industrial archaeology (chapter 8)

○ Other place to visit (chapter 9)

══ Principal road

Malvern Hills Animal & Bird Garden ○

Ha[r]
Ca[r]

A449

Little Malvern ⊞†

A41[]

British Camp ⌂

LEDBURY ●

Midsummer Hill ⌂

Birtsmorton ■†

A438

M50

M50

(2)

0	5	10 kilometres

0	5 miles

WEST MIDLANDS
BIRMINGHAM
HIRE
STOURBRIDGE
A456
Staffs. &
Worcs.
Canal
Hagley Hagley
Hall
Falconry Centre
Clent Hills
Churchill
Forge
Clent
DERMINSTER
Waseley Hill
Stone
Belbroughton
Harvington
Hall
Lickey Hills
Chaddesley
Corbett
Dodford
BROMSGROVE
Lickey
Incline
Hartlebury
Castle
Tardebigge
Locks
Tardebigge
Avoncroft
Museum
Bordesley Abbey
and Forge Mill
Stoke Prior
Stoke Pound
Droitwich
Canals
Stoke Wharf
REDDITCH
ersley
DROITWICH
Stoke Works
Hanbury
Junction
Arrow Valley
Lake
warpe Valley
Nature Trail
Hanbury
Hall
WARWICKSHIRE
alwarpe
Dodderhill
Jinney Ring
Craft Centre
Hawford
Dovecote
Oddingley
Feckenham
CESTER
Tibberton
Bridge
Himbleton
White Cottage
Garden
ALCESTER
arndon
Huddington
Dormston
Inkberrow
Crowle
Spetchley
Abbots
Morton
A46
Worcester
Woods
Spetchley Park
Rous Lench
River Avon
Church Lench
Annard
Woollen Mill
Harvington
Cleeve Prior
Pirton
Windmill Hill
Croome
d'Abitot
PERSHORE
Fladbury
Twyford
Country
Centre
Middle Littleton
Dunstall
Castle Folly
Besford
Wick
Pershore College
of Horticulture
Domestic
Fowl Trust
Eckington
Bridge
Little
Comberton
EVESHAM
Bretforton
Hill Croome
Dovecote
Great
Comberton
Elmley
Castle
Kemerton
Camp
Bredon
Hill
Childswickham
N UPON
ERN
The Priory
Overbury
Broadway
ople
Kemerton
Barnfield
Cider Mill
Fish Hill
shley
Bredon
Beckford
Broadway
Tower
TEWKESBURY
GLOUCESTERSHIRE

Preface

Welcome to the Shire County Guide to Worcestershire, one of over thirty such books, written and designed to enable you to organise your time in the county well.

The Shire County Guides fill the need for a compact, accurate and thorough guide to each county so that visitors can plan a half-day excursion or a whole week's stay to best advantage. Residents, too, will find the guides a handy and reliable reference to the places of interest in their area.

Travelling British roads can be time consuming, and the County Guides will ensure that you need not inadvertently miss any interesting feature in a locality, that you do not accidentally bypass a new museum or an outstanding church, that you can find an attractive place to picnic, and that you will appreciate the history and the buildings of the towns or villages in which you stop.

This book has been arranged in special interest chapters, such as the countryside, historic houses and gardens,or industrial archaeology. and all these places of interest are located on the map on pages 4-5. Use the map either for an overview to decide which area has most to interest you, or to help you enjoy your immediate neighbour-hood. Then refer to the nearest town or village in chapter 2 to see, at a glance, what special features or attractions each community contains or is near. The subsequent chapters enable readers with a particular interest to find immediately those places of importance to them, while the cross-referencing under 'Towns and villages' assists readers with wider tastes to select how best to spend their time.

Wick Manor and the village cross.

1

Worcestershire: a county of contrasts

The landscapes

Worcestershire is a county of contrasts in terms of both natural and human landscapes. In the north the county boundary reaches to the very edge of the sprawling West Midlands conurbation and the steep rise up to the Midlands plateau. Here are the Lickey and Clent hills and the southern end of Staffordshire's Kinver Edge. The powerful river Severn cuts its way out of Shropshire through this northern rim in a steep-sided, well-wooded valley that is, in places, almost a gorge.

To the west of the Severn lies an entirely different landscape: an area of intimate valleys and half-hidden villages that makes up the north-west corner of Worcestershire. Here the often turbulent river Teme, much smaller than the Severn, has to force its way from Shropshire into Worcestershire, creating a delightful valley noted for its orchards and hop growing. The Teme joins the Severn just below Worcester and, in times of flood, colours the Severn a rich red with the load of sandstone it carries.

South of the Teme the land becomes increasingly hilly and wooded until, suddenly, there are the Malverns, that inspiring range of great bare hills that form what must be the most dramatic range in England. This is Worcestershire's western boundary, dividing the county from neighbouring Herefordshire as clearly as if it were a wall. No river pierces these hills: they are Precambrian rocks, the oldest there are, and far too resistant to be breached by the postglacial meltwater torrents which forced the original paths for the Severn and Teme through the softer sandstones to the north.

The Malvern range is 9 miles (15 km) long, highest at its northern end, where Worcestershire Beacon rises to 1380 feet (425 metres). The whole range is visible from the far side of the county and continues, in a series of summits of decreasing height, southwards to Chase End Hill, 620 feet (191 metres), right on the Gloucestershire border.

No such obvious natural barrier marks the southern boundary of Worcestershire. Here the rural landscape of soft Triassic lowlands merges gently southwards into Gloucestershire, a world apart from the industrial fringes in the north of the county. The exception to this gentle transition is in the extreme south-eastern corner of Worcestershire, where the steep escarpment of the Cotswolds rises immediately south of Broadway. Similarly, there is no obvious eastern boundary to Worcestershire. Here again the county's rolling agricultural landscape corresponds to the Warwickshire farmlands to the east.

In contrast to the Severn and Teme, the Warwickshire Avon has no need to force its way into the county. It is a generally leisurely river, making its way into and across south Worcestershire in great sweeping meanders, joining the Severn right on the county boundary at Tewkesbury. This part of Worcestershire is known as the Vale of Evesham; it is one of England's premier horticultural regions, favoured by rich soil and a mild climate, created by warm air funnelled up the Severn estuary from the Gulf Stream.

Horticulture provides a distinctive farming landscape, especially in an area so extensive as the Vale of Evesham. The absence of livestock renders hedgerows and fences largely unnecessary and there are frequent glasshouse complexes and vast orchards. This is in marked contrast to the rest of lowland Worcestershire, which displays the typical Midlands landscape of mixed farming: a pattern of trees, hedgerows and barns which most visitors are happiest to encounter.

There is one other prominent landscape

feature in south Worcestershire: the much loved Bredon Hill. Immortalised by A. E. Housman, it has in recent years inspired local authors Fred Archer and John Moore to write a whole series of novels and reminiscences. Almost circular, Bredon rises steeply from the surrounding lowland and is ringed by delightful villages. Geologically it is an outlier of the nearby Cotswolds: its oolitic limestone gives a softly rounded hill which supports woodlands on its flanks and springy pasture on the undulating summit. Here cattle as well as sheep thrive, in contrast to the bare Malverns, where only sheep grazing is practicable.

One final contrast which may be highlighted is the distribution of towns in Worcestershire. By far the greater part of the population live in the north of the county: in Redditch, Bromsgrove, Droitwich and the three closely grouped towns of Kidderminster, Stourport-on-Severn and Bewdley. Worcester and Great Malvern are the other two major centres of population, both towards the west of the county. South-east Worcestershire, a third of the county's area, contains only Evesham and Pershore, modest settlements on the Avon, and the even smaller Upton upon Severn.

The largest area of continuous woodland in Worcestershire today is Wyre Forest in the north of the county. The landscape the earliest postglacial settlers would have encountered was almost wholly forested, with extensive marshland in the main river valleys. Only the higher summits would have been sparsely provided with trees but they would certainly not be the bare hills we see today. These are the result of centuries of sheep grazing.

The history of Worcestershire

It was on the hills that the major identifiable prehistoric settlements were established. The best, and most accessible, is the multivallate British Camp on Herefordshire Beacon, halfway along the Malvern range. Not so obvious from the eastern side, it can be seen in impressive detail from the western approach road, in Herefordshire. Further south in the range, at Midsummer Hill, there is a second smaller earthwork.

There have been various finds representing most pre-Roman cultures but nothing spectacular. Nor have there been any major Roman discoveries. Droitwich and Worcester were the two main Roman settlements. At Droitwich salt was extracted and distributed along the four saltways radiating from the town: two went north; one due east to Alcester in Warwickshire, where it connected with the north-south Ryknild Street; the fourth went south to Worcester, and onwards eventually to reach Bath. A fairly substantial Roman town seems to have been developed at Worcester with some evidence for an iron-smelting works, a harbour on the Severn, strong fortifications and perhaps an early Christian community.

With the departure of the Roman legions and the Saxon invasion the Severn valley eventually became a territory settled by the Hwicce, who owed allegiance to the Mercian King Penda. St Augustine arrived in the mid seventh century and in 680 the Hwicce were granted their own diocese, centred on Worcester. The early bishops were from St Hilda's at Whitby, North Yorkshire, and they built a wooden cathedral, dedicated to St Mary. The foundations of the abbeys at Pershore and Evesham followed soon after.

The Danes came next, raiding up the Severn, but met stout resistance. There is the story, widely known in Worcester, that they entered the cathedral and stole the sanctus bell. One of the raiding party was captured and the righteous citizens flayed him and nailed his skin to the cathedral door as a warning to any future would-be Danish robbers.

In about 960 St Oswald was appointed bishop and under his direction the monastery extended its influence throughout the diocese; agriculture flourished and the cathedral church of St Mary was considerably enlarged. The west Midlands were divided into shires, each taking its name from its administrative centre: hence Worcestershire.

Four years before the Norman Conquest St Wulfstan became bishop and, as a strong supporter of William of Normandy, he was confirmed in his appointment after 1066, when many Saxon bishops were being replaced by

The memorial cross to the battle of Evesham in All Saints' churchyard, Evesham.

Normans.

To this period belongs the building of the present cathedral, which was consecrated in 1088. Although much has been altered, added to and restored since then, Wulfstan's superb crypt remains virtually unaltered. There followed a century of prolific church building in Worcestershire, and many of these churches can still be seen.

King John had a great affection for Worcester and visited it a number of times. He died in 1216 at Newark-on-Trent in Nottinghamshire and his body was conveyed to Worcester, as was his wish, to be entombed in the cathedral before the high altar. The marble effigy on the tomb cover dates from about 1220 and is the earliest royal effigy in England.

Worcestershire became the centre of affairs briefly in the reign of King John's elder son, Henry III. Henry was never at ease with his barons and open hostility broke out between them, the barons being led by the king's brother-in-law Simon de Montfort. Edward,

Henry's elder son, waged a vigorous campaign against the barons. The final confrontation occurred near Evesham in 1265. Here de Montfort was defeated and killed; his body was buried before the high altar in Evesham Abbey. The modern memorial can be seen in the abbey grounds.

Upheaval did not cease in Worcestershire after 1265. The county was near enough to Wales to suffer a number of incursions from disaffected Celts, particularly during the reign of Henry IV (1399-1413), when Owen Glendower reached as far east as Worcester before being repelled.

No great engagements in the Wars of the Roses (1455-85) took place in Worcestershire but there were members of the powerful Mortimer family at Martley and Hugh Mortimer was killed at Wakefield (1459); his monument is in Martley church. Other prominent residents featured throughout the protracted struggle, including Sir Reginald Bray of Worcester, who distinguished himself at

Bosworth (1485), was knighted on the field and later became Lord Treasurer.

A new dynasty was established when Henry Tudor won the day at Bosworth and was crowned Henry VII: now Worcestershire moves to the very centre of national events. Henry's elder son Prince Arthur was born in 1486 and negotiations began, by the time he was two years old, for him to be married to Princess Catherine of Aragon, daughter of Ferdinand and Isabella of Spain. A royal residence at Bewdley, Tickenhill, was transformed into a magnificent house during Prince Arthur's childhood and here, in 1499, he was married by proxy to Catherine, who had not even arrived in England. When they were eventually united their marriage lasted only a few months before Arthur died, at Ludlow Castle in Shropshire. His body was borne in a great procession to Worcester Cathedral and today we can view the chantry built to house his tomb, which remains impressive despite

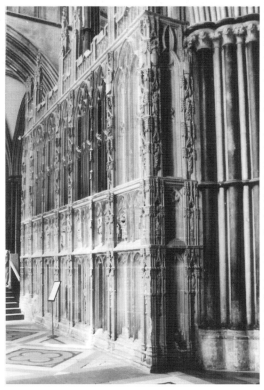

Prince Arthur's chantry in Worcester Cathedral.

being mutilated in the time of Edward VI.

Thus in Worcestershire was set in train events that were to affect the subsequent course of history. Henry, Prince Arthur's younger brother, had been destined to become Archbishop of Canterbury. Instead he married his dead brother's widow by papal dispensation in 1509, after succeeding his father as Henry VIII. Twenty-four years later came the break with Rome as Henry annulled his own marriage and the scene was set for the suppression of England's monastic houses.

The smaller foundations were Henry's first target, in 1536, and present-day Worcestershire was left with only the priories at Worcester and Great Malvern and the abbeys at Pershore and Evesham. The hospitals of St Mary at Droitwich and St Oswald in Worcester also disappeared but the Commandery survived. Many of Worcester's monastic buildings were also spared, as were Great Malvern priory church and much of Pershore abbey church. In the two latter cases, the townspeople were able to raise the money to purchase the churches for parish use. At Evesham there were already two parish churches and the townspeople had no need of a third. The abbey church and all its buildings were therefore demolished, leaving only the great detached bell-tower.

Worcestershire played a prominent role in both the Gunpowder Plot (1605) and the Civil War (1642-51). The county had been a centre for Catholic opposition since the Reformation, a fact which had not escaped Elizabeth I's notice, and there had been several martyrs locally. It is perhaps not surprising therefore that a good deal of the discussion and preparation for the plot to blow up Parliament should have taken place in a Worcestershire house.

Huddington Court lies some 6 miles (10 km) east of Worcester and, in the early seventeenth century, was the home of the Wintour family. Robert Catesby was the prime motivator in the plot and he discussed it with his cousins Thomas and Robert Wintour. Guy

Fawkes was a Yorkshireman enrolled to help implement the plot once it had been planned. Everything went wrong for the conspirators: no one knows exactly why. There are theories concerning betrayal, or government *agents provocateurs*. Whatever the truth, the luckless band fled north-west, through Warwickshire and into Worcestershire, closely pursued by armed men. Resting only briefly once more at Huddington Court, they continued northwards through Hanbury and on to Stourbridge. The pursuit ended at nearby Holbeach Hall, where eight were arrested and subsequently executed. Two priests and a number of other Worcester Catholics were also hanged.

The first and last engagements of the Civil War took place in almost identical locations south of the city of Worcester. The first encounter was little more than a cavalry skirmish centred around Powick Bridge over the river Teme. The Parliamentarians suffered substantial casualties and all the Royalist officers were wounded. Their task was not, however, to defend Worcester but to escort a baggage train of silver plate from Oxford to Charles I at Shrewsbury. This left Worcester open for the Earl of Essex to enter and garrison for Parliament: the small force he left behind soon moved out to Gloucester and the city declared itself for the Royalist cause. It remained thus until the final battle in 1651.

The battle of Worcester was certainly no skirmish. It took place on the meadows where the Teme and Severn join. Charles II had set up his headquarters in Worcester along with his considerably disaffected Scots allies. They were faced with a force of thirty thousand under Oliver Cromwell, who used a flanking movement across the Severn and Teme to break Scottish resistance. The battle swung back and forth throughout the day but finally the Scots were routed and dreadful slaughter took place as they tried to gain refuge in the city through the narrow Sidbury gate. Charles rode along Friar Street to his lodgings on a borrowed horse and managed to leave the city by another gate with a small number of followers, heading for the south coast and nine years' exile in France. The long years of civil strife had ended at Worcester.

Powick Bridge, Worcester, was the site of the first Civil War skirmish. It is dominated by Worcester's first power station, built in 1894.

From then on the Worcestershire we see today evolved. In the eighteenth century Worcester was provided with streets of elegant houses and many of its public buildings and the Georgian towns of Bewdley and Upton upon Severn were established. The canals followed, leading to the creation of Stourport-on-Severn, although only the north of the county was greatly affected by the Industrial Revolution. Worcester became noted for fine porcelain and gloves, Kidderminster became the world's largest carpet-manufacturing town and Great Malvern developed as a fashionable spa.

Today there is all this and much more to see in Worcestershire: a county that mixes its bustling north quite happily with its rural south, its wide Severn lowlands with the hills along its western edges. Worcestershire is a county of contrasts, waiting to be discovered.

2
Towns and villages

Abberley

The steep wooded slope of Abberley Hill provides the backdrop for a little village centre that is nearly perfect. Here, in a garden setting, is the most imaginative and attractive restoration of an ancient church: Norman on a Saxon foundation. Only the chancel remains intact but inside it is beautifully preserved and full of treasures, including a bell brought from Cumberland in 1514. Outside, the ruins of the nave and tower have been transformed into a patio area with a Saxon tomb cover and other memorials displayed. The whole building is surrounded by a garden-like area with lawns and a dovecote shaded by large trees. All this was accomplished by the rector and a band of volunteers in the 1960s. Across the road stands a most attractive village inn, distinguished by its row of painted coats of arms along the façade.

On a hill nearby stands the nineteenth-century church of St Mary; one can walk or drive to it. Built in 1850 and badly damaged by fire in 1876, then subsequently renovated, the church is in the late thirteenth-century Decorated style. Among the notable features are the polished marble columns with finely carved stone capitals, the misericords in the choir stalls, the Ashton engraved memorial window in the north wall and the imposing east window in the chancel. From the churchyard there are extensive views across the rolling countryside in this lovely part of Worcestershire.

On the other side of Abberley Hill, off the A443, is Abberley Hall, now a school. A clock-tower, looking very like Big Ben, protrudes above the trees. Built in 1883, it is a landmark for miles around.

Abberley Hall, page 72.

In the locality: churches at Great Witley, page 61, Rock, page 66, and Stockton on Teme, page 68; Witley Court and Grounds, page 79.

Abbots Morton

This rather remote little village on the eastern boundary of the county is worth seeking out for its remarkable variety of timber-framed buildings, generally maintained to a very high standard; even the postbox opposite the lychgate is thatched! The church of St Peter occupies an elevated position at the western end of the village. Its interior has largely escaped Victorian restoration, with some good woodwork and a pleasant old-world atmosphere.

The neighbouring hamlet of **Radford** is also extremely well-kept. It has an inn and another idiosyncratic postbox: a Victorian one made to look like a miniature timber-framed house.

Alfrick

Church of St Mary Magdalene, page 55; Knapp and Papermill Nature Reserve, page 50; Ravenshill Woodland Nature Reserve, page 50.

Astley

Stanley Baldwin (page 103) died at Astley Hall in 1947. It can be seen across the fields to the east of the church. A lane leads from the church steeply down to a bridge over the Dick Brook and Astley Mill (OS 138: SO 782674), which has been well restored as a private house; an exceptionally high weir gives an impressive fall of water, especially after heavy rain.

Astley Vineyards, page 100; **church of St Peter**, page 55.

Beckford

Beckford Silk Printing Centre, page 100; church of St John the Baptist, page 55.

Belbroughton

Holy Trinity church is on a hillside site at the southern end of the village, built on an

The town centre and St Anne's church at Bewdley.

exposure of the underlying Old Red Sandstone. The large north aisle and chapel, almost as big as the nave and chancel, give the impression of two churches side by side. There is old glass in the north aisle; the south-aisle windows are nineteenth-century and the lively south chancel window dates from 1905. The Jacobean pulpit has beasts, probably dragons, carried round the top.

The church is surrounded by a number of substantial Georgian buildings and opposite is the village school of 1876. Down the hill is the much busier part of the village, with an enjoyable variety of buildings of various ages.

In the locality: Clent church, page 56; Clent Hills Country Park, page 45.

Besford
Church of St Peter, page 56.

Bewdley
Bewdley was established as a port on the river Severn in medieval times, receiving its charter from Edward IV in 1472. By the mid eighteenth century it was thriving as the centre of most water-borne traffic on the upper Severn. The rejection, in the 1760s, of James Brindley's plan to terminate his Staffordshire & Worcestershire Canal at Bewdley led to the establishment of Stourport a short distance downstream. From then on, Bewdley declined as a transport centre as river cargo moved to the new complex at the upstart Stourport and finally disappeared almost completely with the advent of railways.

In the prosperous years before trade declined, however, the delightful Georgian town we can enjoy today was created. Bewdley lies along the west bank of the Severn; the suburb of Wribbenhall is opposite, and the two are joined by a fine Telford bridge completed in 1800. There is a car park just upstream from the bridge.

Thomas Telford's bridge is the ideal starting point to take one's bearings and plan an exploration of the town. Both upstream and downstream lie the former quay areas with mainly Georgian buildings creating an extremely satisfying riverside street. Ahead the broad width of Load Street climbs uphill towards the tall tower of St Anne's church. Before leaving the bridge, turn to look at the attractive riverside frontage of Wribbenhall on the east bank, with its pleasant mixture of Georgian and earlier timber-framed buildings.

Halfway up Load Street, on the left, is the neo-classical town hall of 1808. This conceals the almost unique Shambles, a narrow brick-paved street entirely lined by former butchers' premises. This houses the fascinating Bewdley Museum, which records the town's history and relationship with the surrounding area, particularly the Wyre Forest (page 47).

St Anne's church stands in the centre of the main crossroads, without surrounding churchyard: it is very much a town church. The tall west tower dates from 1748; the remainder of the building is fifty years later. Major restoration work in 1992-3 has created an interior of wonderful spaciousness and light. Of particular interest are the modern chandeliers; the motifs etched into their curving glass panels complement those decorating the north and south windows.

The lesser streets of the town centre well repay exploring. They are full of delightful buildings of various styles and periods and interesting little shops.

Bewdley was the birthplace of Stanley Baldwin (page 103).

Across the river in Wribbenhall is the Bewdley station of the Severn Valley steam railway, with a large car park.

Bewdley Museum, page 83; **Severn Valley Railway**, page 101.

In the locality: Blackstone Meadows Country Park, page 45; Devil's Spittleful and Rifle Range Nature Reserve, page 50; Habberley Valley, page 49; Rock church, page 66; Seckley Wood and Hawkbatch Valleys, page 47; West Midlands Safari and Leisure Park, page 102; Wyre Forest Visitor Centre, page 47.

Birtsmorton

Moated Birtsmorton Court (not open) is one of Worcestershire's most picturesque houses, surpassed probably only by Huddington Court (page 29). The oldest parts of the house are the two bastions and archway of the four-

teenth century. The Nanfan family lived here and Cardinal Wolsey was chaplain and tutor early in his career. Much later it was the home of William Huskisson MP, who had the dubious distinction of being the first person ever to be killed in a railway accident, at the opening of George Stephenson's Liverpool & Manchester Railway in 1830.

Church of St Peter and St Paul, page 56.

Bredon

This highly attractive village has most of the elements for an enjoyable visit: picturesque cottages, village inn, thirteenth-century tithe barn, riverside walks and a fine church with an Elizabethan rectory.

The large church of St Giles has a battlemented tower topped by a graceful spire 160 feet (49 metres) high. Unusually, the aisles run only half the length of the nave and can more appropriately be termed chapels. The central tower is not flanked by transepts and the chancel is almost as long as the nave. The upper storey of the vaulted Norman north porch was a parvise with access by ladder. The west end is also Norman but the rest of the building is fourteenth-century except for the thirteenth-century south aisle.

This aisle is known as the Mitton Chapel and has three tombs in arched recesses. One has a shield with two arms curved round holding a heart and is said to contain the heart of a knight killed on a crusade. The chapel also contains the magnificent alabaster effigies of Sir Giles and Lady Catherine Reed, erected in 1611. Black marble columns support an ornate canopy featuring the family arms flanked by marble obelisks and small figures. The couple's eight children in miniature kneel facing them.

The village contains numerous enjoyable buildings. Near the church are the Elizabethan stone rectory, the seventeenth-century Old Mansion and the eighteenth-century Manor House. Particularly imposing is the range of eighteenth-century stables opposite the church. Along the main street are Hancock's Endowed School (1845) and the single-storey Reed Almshouses (1696).

The great timber-framed tithe or manorial barn lies along a lane west of the church and is National Trust property.

Bredon Barn, page 51; **Bredon Hill**, page 49.

In the locality: Kemerton Camp, page 52; The Priory, Kemerton, page 78.

Bretforton

The village is centred on its square, with church, school, shops and an ancient village inn, the Fleece, important enough to be in the care of the National Trust. The Manor House dates originally from 1600, with subsequent additions, and there is a good mixture of timber-framed and stone houses throughout the village.

The church of St Leonard is crowded around with tombstones and yew trees which make an overall view rather difficult. It has a tall fifteenth-century tower and a chancel unusually somewhat longer than the nave. The Norman arcades have lively and intricate capital decorations, particularly St Margaret being swallowed by a dragon. Undaunted, however, she has used her cross to cut open its side and is about to re-emerge.

Some windows show pastoral scenes, as befits a prime agricultural area, and in the south transept or chapel are seventeenth-century panels carved with leaf and other patterns.

Fleece Inn, page 51.

In the locality: Domestic Fowl Trust, page 100.

Broadway

Visitors to Broadway in the holiday season are strongly advised to arrive early, such is the popularity of this beautiful village. It is a village of the Vale of Evesham but its appearance is pure Cotswold: its main street at the eastern end reaches to the very foot of the 450 feet (140 metres) high Cotswold escarpment. Somehow Broadway manages to cope with its never ending popularity: its greens, gardens and buildings are beautifully maintained. The shops, galleries and catering establishments range from the popular to the highly exclusive.

The wide village green is a good vantage point. Around it are highly individualistic buildings – inns, shops and private houses –

but all given unity by the honey-coloured oolitic limestone which is their common building material. The only exception is the delightful timber-framed wing of the Broadway Hotel behind its carefully clipped yew.

Beyond the green the main street is tree-lined. The Lygon Arms, Picton House, Tudor House, the new development of Cotswold Court and a row of delightful bow-windowed shops, some thatched, are among the features of the streetscape. As the street starts to rise there are fine art and antique galleries and the entertaining Broadway Teddy Bear Museum.

Along a road leading from the green is St Michael's church of 1839, considerably restored in 1890. The entrance is in the tall tower, under an organ loft. Both aisles contain fairly modern windows: those in the chancel are much better, one unusual in depicting St Elizabeth of Hungary. The intricately carved Elizabethan wooden pulpit came from the old St Eadburga's church, installed here as a thanksgiving for the end of the First World War. St Eadburga's church is usually open in the summer months. Originally Norman, it was much altered up to the fourteenth

The church of St Leonard at Bretforton.

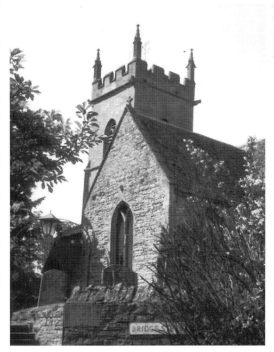

century, when the lower stages of the crossing tower were constructed. The pulpit has panels from a chapel which was on the site of St Michael's church. There is a screen made from old bench ends and a Jacobean communion rail. Fragments of old glass are in several windows.

Barnfield Cider Mill, page 100; **Broadway Teddy Bear Museum**, page 83; **Broadway Tower Country Park**, page 45; **Fish Hill**, page 49.

Bromsgrove

Bromsgrove Museum and tourist information centre are at the north end of the High Street, with a convenient car park opposite. Bromsgrove was an important staging post on the Birmingham to Bristol road but its High Street has now been fortunately bypassed and the north end pedestrianised. As in many towns, it is the upper storeys, above the shop fascias, which tell the story of the town: Victorian, Georgian and the occasional timber-framed frontage can be seen here. In the street are two modern statues: the Dryad and Boar, and A. E. Housman (page 105).

Beyond the pedestrianised area New Road enters High Street. Number 1 New Road is the Hop Pole Inn, moved here and rebuilt in the 1860s. The original building dates from 1572: the builder's initials and the date are on the façade, which has been somewhat altered from its original form and given a rather startling Victorian porch.

There is another good timber-framed building on the corner of Market Place. Here turn right and cross the inner ring road to the steps up to the red sandstone church, with the lychgate at the top. Walk left and enter by the twelfth-century south porch. Above the entrance is a statue of St John the Baptist, to whom the church is dedicated.

An impressive building by parish-church standards, two features are of particular note: the stained glass windows, which are all nineteenth-century; and, particularly, the rich collection of monuments. Especially notable are those in the chantry chapel: Sir John Talbot (1550) and his two wives, Margaret and Elizabeth; Sir Humphrey Stafford (1450) and his wife Alianora. Both these monuments are in a superb state of preservation and The

Bromsgrove's Market Place and the spire of the church of St John the Baptist.

Summertime on Bredon Hill.

Wisteria flowering in Broadway village.

show finely detailed carving.

In the chancel are the alabaster monument to Lady Elizabeth Talbot (1517), with superb costume detail, and above it the memorial to Bishop John Hall of Bristol (1710), a former vicar of Bromsgrove. On the south wall is the memorial to Benjamin Maude, a noted local botanist. The intricately carved organ screen, depicting many figures with local connections, and the modern memorial pulpit should also be seen.

In the churchyard are interesting tombs worth seeking out, especially the much defaced and weathered chest tomb of a knight beside the main path on the north side and the two headstones to engineers who were killed on the Lickey Incline in 1840 when the locomotive they were driving blew up. From here there is a gently sloping path down to the ring road, past the dignified and effective Burma Campaign Monument of 1982.

Bromsgrove Museum, page 85; **Lickey Incline**, page 98.

In the locality: Avoncroft Museum of Historic Buildings, pages 85 and 97; Hanbury Hall, page 75; Jinney Ring Craft Centre, page 101; Lickey Hills Country Park, page 46; Stoke Pound, page 97; Stoke Wharf, page 97; Stoke Works, page 97; Tardebigge Locks and Wharf, page 97; Waseley Hill Country Park, page 47; and churches at Dodford, page 58; Stoke Prior, page 68; and Tardebigge, page 69.

Bushley

Near the church are a number of interesting houses and cottages and a short distance west is Bushley Green, a delightful picnic spot with cricket pitch and pavilion, and footpaths setting off across the surrounding countryside.

Church of St Peter, page 18.

Chaddesley Corbett

This is a village to delight the visitor, with an immaculate church and churchyard, well-maintained buildings and numerous attractive gardens.

Cottages in Chaddesley Corbett.

The village green and the church of St Andrew at Cleeve Prior.

church is dedicated to St Cassian, who was born in Alexandria in the fifth or sixth century and became bishop of an African diocese. The chancel is Worcestershire's most striking example of the Decorated style of the early fourteenth century. It is brightly lit by an impressive five-light east window with particularly intricate tracery. On the wall is the sixteenth-century Forest family brass.

Two archways separate the chancel from St Nicholas's Chapel, which contains monuments on the north wall and, under one arch, a worn effigy of a priest. Another effigy, of a knight in armour, probably late thirteenth-century, is in the south aisle. Both aisles have nineteenth-century windows and the middle window of the north aisle is by A. J. Davies of the Bromsgrove Guild (1926). Particularly notable is the Norman font of about 1160. Its bulky bowl is deeply carved, with a frieze of intricate plaiting above fearsome dragons.

The churchyard contains numerous large chest tombs shaded by yews. Along one side is a school building, restored and enlarged in 1809. Nearby is the early Georgian Lychgate House and, across the road, the Talbot Inn, a fine timber-framed hostelry of the sixteenth and seventeenth centuries. From here the whole village street is worth exploring.

In the locality: Harvington Hall, page 76.

Childswickham

The original village centre around the church is delightful and well worth seeking out behind the large area of modern development. The tall church tower with its slender spire is a landmark to follow: a footpath from the churchyard leads across a stream and provides a circular walk round the village, including the green with its stepped cross surmounted by an urn.

In the locality: Barnfield Cider Mill, page 100.

Churchill

Churchill Forge, page 98.

Church Lench

Annard Woollen Mill, page 100; church of All Saints, page 56.

Cleeve Prior

The village green is a pleasant setting with thatched cottages of stone, brick and timber framing. Further along the street, next to the inn, the Old Cider Mill, now a house, is decorated with antique farm implements.

Church of St Andrew, page 56; **Cleeve Prior Nature Reserve**, page 50.

Clent

Clent is a delightful hillside area but a village centre is hard to define. Its houses are scattered

Above: *Chateau Impney near Droitwich, built for John Corbett in 1875.*
Left: *The black and white tower of St Nicholas's church at Dormston.*

along the street to the left of the church, many of them amongst trees. Outside the church, to the left of the lychgate, is the former village school with an open bell-tower on top. It has been very well converted to a private house and a plaque records an award for this.

Church of St Leonard, page 56; **Clent Hills Country Park**, page 45.

Clifton upon Teme

This is a most enjoyable village, not actually on the Teme, but in the lovely hilly country to the west of the river. The church of St Kenelm stands among yews and shrubs overlooking a number of interesting chest tombs and a large churchyard cross. The tower, nave and chancel date from about 1200 and the south aisle from the fourteenth century. There is an effigy of a knight, probably Sir Ralph Wysham who died in 1332, and a lead-lined font which still has the staple from the time when it was locked to prevent the holy water being used for witchcraft.

The village well repays a leisurely stroll.

The fine inn next to the church retains an original circular AA sign on its wall; opposite is the village green with the school on the far side. Around the green and all along the main street is a variety of delightful houses – timber-framed, brick of various ages, a stone cottage and, unusually for Worcestershire, one that is weatherboarded.

In the locality: churches at Shelsley Beauchamp, page 67; and Shelsley Walsh, page 67.

Croome d'Abitot
Church of St Mary Magdalene, page 57.

Crowle
Church of St John the Baptist, page 58.

Dodderhill
Church of St Augustine, page 58.

Dodford
Church of Holy Trinity and St Mary, page 58.

Victoria Square and the Raven Hotel, Droitwich Spa.

Dormston

Church of St Nicholas, page 59; Dormston Dovecote, page 51.

Droitwich Spa

The Romans called the town *Salinae* ('salt springs') and roads to carry the salt away radiated from here, making it one of Britain's most important production centres in Roman times. Salt production continued throughout the centuries and became a highly organised industry in the nineteenth century under John Corbett (page 103), who moved salt production to Stoke Prior (page 97). He subsequently established Droitwich as a fashionable spa resort for taking the salt waters. His house, the incredibly ornate French Renaissance Château Impney, now an hotel, is on the A38 just north-east of Droitwich.

Today the salt industry and much of the spa's function have gone, but there remain a number of interesting buildings and locations within the town to recall those days. The Heritage Centre provides a useful starting point for understanding the town's development and for a walk around historic Droitwich. A booklet is available guiding the visitor around the most important buildings, which include the Raven Hotel, the former town hall, the Old Cock Inn, Salters' Hall and the Brine Baths.

In the centre of the town is St Andrew's church, founded in the thirteenth century and now rather squat in appearance owing to the removal of the upper half of its tower because of subsidence. The chancel is small but with an impressive east window, which is a First World War monument. Of the numerous wall tablets, the most impressive is the Coningsby memorial (1734) on the massive pillar supporting the tower. The north-east chapel, commissioned in 1262, is dedicated to St Richard de Wyche (1197-1253), a native of Droitwich who subsequently became Bishop of Chichester. It is thought that pilgrims used to view relics of the saint through a narrow opening which still exists between the chancel and this chapel.

High Street, semi-pedestrianised, runs beside the church. It is hard to believe that this street was level earlier in the twentieth century. Salt extraction has caused subsidence and some of the older buildings are leaning at a marked angle. Halfway along, in Gurneys Lane, is the site of the last salt works in Droitwich.

Along the Worcester Road, on the outskirts of Droitwich, is the Catholic Church of the Sacred Heart. It was built in the early 1930s in a markedly Italian style, with a tall campanile. Inside, the church is remarkable for its mosaics created from 8 tonnes of tiny squares of Venetian glass. These are considered to be the finest mosaics in Great Britain apart from Westminster Cathedral. Particularly notable are the seven panels in the nave chronicling the life of St Richard.

Droitwich Canals, page 95; **Droitwich Spa Heritage Centre**, page 86; **Salwarpe Valley Nature Trails**, page 49.

In the locality: Hanbury Hall, page 75; Hanbury Junction, page 97; Jinney Ring Craft Centre, page 101; and churches at Dodderhill, page 58; Himbleton, page 62; Oddingley, page 65; and Salwarpe, page 67.

Eckington

Eckington Bridge Picnic Site, page 49.

Elmley Castle

The tree-lined village street leading up to the church is a delight with its variety of attractive houses and stream along one side. The eleventh-century castle, which stood well above the village, has long since gone. It was the home of the Beauchamps, the county's leading family, but they removed to neighbouring Warwickshire and the castle was in decay from the sixteenth century.

St Mary's church has a tree-shaded setting. On the left of the path is a complicated sundial of the sixteenth or seventeenth century. The battlemented stone porch contains occasional carved stones including a lively rabbit: nearby Bredon Hill has long been noted for its rabbit population. The chancel, which is possibly eleventh-century, has a fine barrel roof and there are good windows, particularly the east window of 1875 and those on both sides of the chancel. The finest features, however, are the seventeenth-century Savage and Coventry monuments in the side chapel, which are among the best in Worcestershire. In the nave are pleasantly hewn old pews and

the font is octagonal with superbly carved dragons on the base.

In the locality: Bredon Hill, page 49; Kemerton Camp, page 52.

Evesham

Located in a great meander of the river Avon, Evesham is a busy market town which grew up beside a major monastery. This was a Benedictine house, founded in 714 by St Ecgwine of Worcester, bishop of the Hwicce. The foundation attracted valuable gifts of large tracts of land in the Avon valley, Feckenham Forest and on the Cotswold uplands. The income from these lands financed successive phases of building right up to the early sixteenth century, not long before the Dissolution.

Ecgwine's church collapsed around 960 and another was built, to be replaced by a third, larger church which was consecrated in 1054. Around 1080 the first Norman abbot, Walter, began a yet greater church, which needed a century for its completion.

The bell-tower of the former abbey at Evesham.

A village street at Elmley Castle.

The Winter Gardens at Great Malvern.

The abbey gateway in Evesham leads to the Market Place.

Successive abbots added steadily to the extent and amenities of the domestic buildings: Abbot Clement Lichfield, the last abbot before the Dissolution, was particularly noted as a patron of architecture.

The market town to the north of the abbey precincts was created by the abbots in the eleventh century. It was divided into two parishes, for which two parish churches were built within the precincts: St Lawrence and All Saints. As a result the townspeople had no need of the great abbey church after the Dissolution: it was demolished along with almost all the domestic buildings.

Impressive buildings remain, however: the bell-tower 110 feet (35 metres) high (1524-32); the Almonry (part fourteenth-century), now a museum; the town gateway (1139-43), with later timber-framed work; and the Free School (1513-24), of which the original porch survives. Visitors are recommended to study the excellent model in the Almonry to appreciate the full extent of the monastic complex at the time of suppression in 1540.

It was the meander of the Avon that proved Simon de Montfort's undoing in the Barons' War. Here he was trapped and defeated by royalist forces in the battle of Evesham (1265). His dismembered body was buried before the high altar in the abbey church: the site is marked by a large ornamental stone in what is now the Abbey Gardens.

The Market Place immediately north of the monastic area has numerous interesting timber-framed and later, mainly Georgian buildings. The narrow street leading into the Market Place has a long jettied timber-framed building, possibly the bead-houses erected in the time of Abbot Zattoni (1379-1418). In the Market Place is the late fifteenth-century Booth Hall with closely set timbered uprights and two jettied upper storeys. Nearby are the later library, town hall and market hall.

The High Street is wide and fairly long, attesting to its former use as an extension of the market area. Dresden House (Number 51) is particularly notable: dated 1692, it is a wide house with large iron brackets either side of the front door. There are a number of substantial Georgian town houses either side of the street.

Bridge Street leads from the Market Place down to the Workman Bridge, named after a former mayor. From here pleasant riverside gardens border the Avon and one can walk through a park back up to the monastic precincts. Pleasure pools mark the line of the former fishponds of the monastery.

Almonry Heritage Centre, page 86; **church of All Saints**, page 59; **church of St Lawrence**, page 59; **Twyford Country Centre**, page 102.

In the locality: Annard Woollen Mill, page 100; Domestic Fowl Trust, page 100; the Fleece Inn, Bretforton, page 51; Middle Littleton Tithe Barn, page 53; Windmill Hill Nature Reserve, page 50; and churches at Church Lench, page 56; Cleeve Prior, page 56; Harvington, page 62; and Middle Littleton, page 65.

Feckenham

Feckenham originally lay in the extensive Royal Forest of Feckenham and a manor much used by twelfth- and thirteenth-century kings was located here. The manor has gone and only fragments of the forest survive. Today Feckenham is a fairly large, very attractive village located on the Roman Saltway (now B4090) midway between Droitwich and Alcester in Warwickshire. The High Street leaves the main road at right angles and virtually the whole length of the street has a delightful mixture of timber-framed and brick houses, several being exceptionally good examples of Georgian architecture.

The High Street widens out to a square and the church of St John the Baptist lies to the left. It is predominantly Victorian in external appearance with a large west tower, approached through a well-maintained churchyard, including a pretty rockery at the gate – a present from the people of the village to a local lady on her hundredth birthday.

Inside the church the nave and chancel both have painted ceilings between the beams, and the north aisle has painted arches. The roof beams of the nave end in a series of carved stone figures, apparently angels. On the chancel north wall is a monument of 1823 showing a young woman leaning on a plinth and holding a child on her left arm. The north-aisle altar is a splendid antique refectory table with a wooden backing decorated with painted coats of arms; above it is a good stained glass window of 1904 and on the adjacent north wall are three wall monuments.

In the churchyard are a preaching cross and some good chest tombs.

Fladbury

An attractive village on the river Avon, Fladbury has a large village green with a good evergreen oak. In the main street there is a variety of attractive houses, especially Brook Manor, of around 1700, with heraldic beasts on its gate pillars and urns on the façade pediment.

Halfway along the street, the church of St John the Baptist stands in a large churchyard. The entrance porch has rib vaulting and previously included an upper storey. Inside, the

Georgian ceiling of the nave has fine moulded centrepieces. Of the monuments, the Throckmorton brasses of 1445 are notable. Particularly noteworthy are the large number of stained glass windows: the older are superior, especially the Virgin and Child in the vestry and the shields in the chancel, both fourteenth- century.

Great Comberton
Church of St Michael, page 60.

Great Malvern

The lower eastern slopes of the Malvern Hills are the enviable setting for this delightful town. Great Malvern is the largest of six linked settlements. Malvern Wells and Little Malvern are to the south; North and West Malvern to the north and Malvern Link on the lowlands to the north-east. This sounds like urban sprawl but there is such variety of landscape and a profusion of open commons and trees that one is unaware of the overall size of the Malverns.

Great Malvern was for many centuries a modest settlement surrounding its priory. The medicinal properties of its spring waters were realised in the seventeenth century but it did not become a fashionable spa resort until Dr John Wall, founder of Worcester Porcelain, published a treatise in 1756 extolling the virtues of the pure Malvern Wells springs. By the early nineteenth century a pump room, baths and several hotels had been established and a guide for visitors published.

Serious promotion of the town as a health resort started in 1842 with the arrival of two doctors, Gully and Wilson. The latter introduced the new concepts of German hydropathy, which gained immense popularity. The arrival of the railway in 1858 provided a further boost to Malvern's development. The town became noted for its educational establishments; Malvern College was founded in 1862.

Malvern was, therefore, a latecomer to the ranks of fashionable spa towns. Hence one finds not Regency crescents and terraces like those of Bath and Cheltenham but the far more varied and individualistic architecture of Victorian times: innumerable large

Diminutive Dexter cattle on parade at the Three Counties Show at Great Malvern.

detached houses in spacious grounds and hotels to cater for the Victorians who flocked to Malvern as it became established.

Two annual events attract large numbers of visitors to Great Malvern: the Malvern Festival in May and the Three Counties Show in June. The festival is centred on the Winter Gardens complex in the town centre which houses a concert hall, theatre and cinema looking out over pleasant gardens. Founded in 1929, the festival staged the premieres of several plays by George Bernard Shaw, and Elgar conducted some of his own compositions here in the 1930s. Today the festival features its own specially commissioned musical works and also attracts a wide variety of fringe events.

The Three Counties Show is one of England's leading agricultural events and is held on a permanent site on the flat lowland below Great Malvern. One of the most attractive showgrounds, with its backdrop of the Malvern Hills, the site is also the setting for other shows and events throughout the year.

Great Malvern's Norman Priory Church is in a tree-shaded setting in the town centre. Nearby are Malvern Museum, the Abbey Gatehouse and the Abbey Hotel (1849). The town and its neighbouring settlements repay endless exploration on foot and by car, particularly Great Malvern's Victorian railway station (1861), with its beautifully painted floral capitals on the cast-iron pillars, and the churches of Little Malvern.

Malvern Hills, page 47; **Malvern Museum**, page 86; **Priory Church of St Mary and St Michael**, page 60.

In the locality: British Camp, page 51; Little Malvern church, page 64; Malvern Hills Animal and Bird Garden, page 101.

Great Witley

Church of St Michael, page 61; Witley Court and Grounds, page 79.

In the locality: Abberley Hall, page 72; Eastgrove Cottage Garden, page 73; churches at Astley, page 55; and Stockton on Teme, page 68.

Hagley

Church of St John the Baptist, page 62; the Falconry Centre (Hagley), page 101. Hagley Hall, page 74.

In the locality: Churchill Forge, page 98; Clent church, page 56; Clent Hills Country Park, page 45.

Overbury village, looking towards Overbury Court.

Walking in the Wyre Forest.

Hanbury

Hanbury Hall, page 75; Hanbury Junction, page 97; Jinney Ring Centre, page 101.

Hanley Castle

The castle has long since disappeared, its site marked only by a moat, but the delightful little village remains, grouped around the churchyard entrance. The diminutive village square has a great cedar as its centrepiece and the unusually named Three Kings Inn, with its sign of the Three Wise Men. There is a pleasing variety of timber-framed and brick-built cottages and the churchyard is partly enclosed by a row of almshouses of 1600 and other ancient cottages. The old grammar school, founded in 1544, is retained as the frontage for a much larger school.

The church of St Mary is large and interesting from the outside. Its nave and aisle are stone-built and the central tower, chancel and north chapel are all of brick, added in 1674. The interior has some enjoyable nineteenth-century windows and monuments to members of the Lechmere family in a side chapel.

There are a number of attractive timber-framed cottages in the neighbouring countryside. Opposite the turning off the B4211 to the village is the impressive gateway and lodge to Severn End and its park: much of the house was destroyed by fire in 1896.

Two miles (3 km) north-west is the neighbouring village of **Hanley Swan**. Its village green, large duck pond and inn make a picturesque spot to linger. There is a signpost to the nearby Catholic Church of Our Lady and St Alphonsus built in 1846, an unusually spacious and well-designed building for its period.

Hartlebury

Hartlebury Castle State Rooms, page 76; Hereford and Worcester County Museum, page 87; Leapgate Country Park, page 46.

Harvington

(near Evesham)

The main street of the village is worth walking along for its pleasant timber-framed houses. If followed to the end, where it is closed off at the bypass, the two most picturesque houses will be found, one thatched and one cruck-built.

Church of St James, page 62.

Harvington

(near Kidderminster)

Harvington Hall, page 76.

Hawford

Hawford Dovecote, page 52.

Hill Croome

Hill Croome Dovecote, page 52.

Himbleton

A footpath at the rear of the churchyard sets off across meadows and two bridges; to the right is a well-preserved timber-framed dovecote. Follow the footpath and turn right at the road for a circular walk around the village.

About 1 mile (2 km) north at a crossroads (OS 150: SO 953597) are Shell Cottage and Shell Manor Farm, both fifteenth-century, and a rare small packhorse bridge beside an often deep ford.

Church of St Mary Magdalene, page 62.

Hollybush

Midsummer Hill, page 53.

Holt

Church of St Martin, page 62; Holt Castle, page 52.

Honeybourne

Domestic Fowl Trust, page 100.

Huddington

The view that greets the visitor is memorable: little St James's church is to the left across a lawn; straight ahead is Huddington Court, the most picturesque house in Worcestershire and one of the most picturesque in England. The house (not open) is timber-framed with superb ornate Tudor chimneys; the gardens, with topiary and dovecote, are immaculate; the moat surrounding the house makes the scene idyllic. Cars should be left on the public road; here there is an unspoilt cruck cottage retaining its original roof line, a prime example of a well preserved but not over-restored Worcestershire cottage.

Church of St James, page 63.

The dovecote in the gardens of Huddington Court.

Inkberrow

Church of St Peter, page 63.
In the locality: Dormston church, page 59;
Dormston Dovecote, page 51; White
Cottage Garden, page 79.

Kemerton

This long village runs up the southern flank of Bredon Hill. At the northern end, where the road starts to climb steeply, is the Priory, a house whose gardens are open during the summer months; a wall of the former priory is preserved as a garden feature.

Kemerton Camp, page 52; **The Priory**, page 78.

Kidderminster

A busy industrial town, Kidderminster is noted for being one of the world's leading centres for carpet manufacturing. Cloth weaving was introduced as early as the fourteenth century by Flemish weavers and became the town's staple industry. Carpet production commenced when John Broom established

the first handloom and made and lost three fortunes trying to establish the trade. The first factory was opened in 1735. Admirers of industrial architecture will find numerous buildings of interest, particularly Brinton's carpet factory near the town hall.

Kidderminster's best-known son, Sir Rowland Hill (page 104), is commemorated by a statue (1881) in front of the town hall (1877), which is worth entering for its opulent ground-floor assembly room and the William Hill organ, unique in remaining in its original condition and location.

From here pedestrianised Vicar Street leads to the Bull Ring and Church Street, which is lined with pleasant Georgian houses. The exception is Number 12, halfway up, which is timber-framed, three-storeyed with leaded windows, a rare survival of pre-Victorian Kidderminster.

Church Street ends at the inner ring road and a subway leads to St Mary's church, prominently sited on a hill overlooking the town. This is Worcestershire's largest parish church, full of interest for the visitor. Outside, facing the town, are the imposing nineteenth-century entrance gates, surmounted by intricate cast-iron scrollwork. There are two statues: one of Richard Baxter, a preacher here in the Civil War period who spoke out against idle clergy; the other a prominent bronze of an angel and child, a First World War memorial.

From the statues steps lead down through a garden to a lock and the towpath of the Staffordshire & Worcestershire Canal, a favourite mooring place for pleasure craft. Also in the neighbourhood are the Kidderminster Railway Museum and the Severn Valley Railway station on Comberton Hill.

Church of St Mary, page 63; **Kidderminster Railway Museum**, page 87; **Severn Valley Railway**, page 101; **Staffordshire & Worcestershire Canal**, page 95.

In the locality: Churchill Forge, page 98; Devil's Spittleful and Rifle Range Nature Reserve, page 50; the Falconry Centre (Hagley), page 101; Habberley Valley, page 49; Hagley Hall, page 74; Hartlebury Castle State Rooms, page 76; Harvington Hall, page 76; Hereford and Worcester County Museum, page 87; Kingsford Country Park, page 46; Koi Water Gardens, page 77; Stone House Cottage Garden, page 79; West Midlands Safari Park, page 102; and churches at Stone, page 69; and Wilden, page 70.

Kingsford

Kingsford Country Park, page 46.

Kyre

Kyre Park, page 77.

Leigh

Church of St Eadburga, page 64; Leigh Court Barn, page 52.

Lickey

Lickey Hills Country Park, page 46.

Little Comberton

Church of St Peter, page 64.

The founder of the penny postage, Sir Rowland Hill, stands outside the town hall in Kidderminster.

Little Malvern

The southernmost of the six Malvern settlements, the village occupies a delightful position at the foot of a particularly steep and heavily wooded slope of the Malvern Hills, looking out eastwards across the Severn lowlands. Sir Edward Elgar (page 103), his wife and their daughter are buried at St Wulstan's Roman Catholic church, on the A449 running along the top of the village. Other notable buildings are Little Malvern Court and the Priory Church of St Giles.

British Camp, page 51; **Little Malvern Court**, page 78; **Priory Church of St Giles**, page 64.

Little Witley

Eastgrove Cottage Garden, page 73.

Lower Broadheath

Elgar Birthplace Museum, page 88.

Above: *Timber-framing in Ombersley.*
Left: *Worcester Cathedral from Fort Royal Hill.*

Martley

Church of St Peter, page 64.
In the locality: Wichenford Dovecote, page 54.

Middle Littleton

Church of St Nicholas, page 65; Middle Littleton Tithe Barn, page 53; Windmill Hill Nature Reserve, page 50.

Oddingley

Church of St James, page 65.

Ombersley

This is a delightful village, once an important coaching stage, now happily bypassed by the A449 Worcester to Kidderminster road. The church of St Andrew (rebuilt 1825-9) stands in a very large churchyard which is full of interesting tombs. Part of the chancel of the old church was retained as the mausoleum of the Sandys family and stands to the south-west. Beyond, from the corner of the church-yard, is a view of Ombersley Court, the home of the Sandys family. It was built in 1726 and refaced with stone in 1814.

The church is entered by a vestibule under the great west tower. The western end of the nave is separated from the body of the church by a glass screen. Notice the 'free seats' on the right inside the door. The interior is rather plain, with a gallery around three sides containing the organ at the west end. The Sandys family pew with its fireplace is in the south aisle. An interesting fitment in the north aisle is the tall iron stove in the fashion of a Gothic church tower. Some windows contain stained glass from the original church.

A short street leads to the south entrance of the churchyard. On the corner is a charity school of 1729 with a Dutch gable at its north end. Two inns lie opposite: a timber-framed building and a late seventeenth-century one with five rounded gables. Both sides of the street have varied buildings as far as the roundabout and just beyond are two good cruck-built houses facing each other.

In the locality: Hawford Dovecote, page 52; Holt Castle, page 52; Holt church, page 62.

Overbury

The church, the village and the setting are as nearly perfect as one could reasonably demand. The village has a wealth of good buildings of varying periods and styles, but the dominant effect is Cotswold, especially around the church. A street leads up the hill with numerous individually interesting houses along one side.

Both churchyard and church are full of interest and both are beautifully maintained. The lychgate of heavy curved timbers by Sir Herbert Baker is a memorial to those who fell in two world wars. On the right a clear stream makes its way across a corner of the churchyard. To the left, beyond a huge magnolia, are a memorial garden and delightful cloisters recording those whose ashes are interred here.

The engraved glass doors of 1973 open into a superb Norman nave with typical short rounded pillars, prominent capitals and semi-circular arches, above which are a particularly fine series of Norman windows. High up above the pulpit is the door which formerly gave access to the rood loft. The carving on both pulpit and pews is worthy of close examination. In the south aisle the font is of a deep goblet design, Norman with later renovation.

Two arches lead under the tower to the Early English chancel and the east window, which has eight lights spanning the width of the wall. The rib-vaulted roof has intricate bosses and carved capitals on the columns. Visitors should not miss the lovely window to St Faith, to whom the church is dedicated. Both church and village are worthy of leisurely inspection: this is one of Worcestershire's most delightful villages. Of particular note are the village hall (1896) by Norman Shaw and the nearby Georgian Red House.

In the locality: Beckford church, page 55; Beckford Silk Printing Centre, page 100; The Priory, Kemerton, page 78.

Pershore

The town originally grew up around its great abbey and the streets in the vicinity still contain a number of timber-framed buildings from medieval Pershore. In the eighteenth century the town developed as a staging post, market centre and crossing point of the river Avon. Thus the overall impression in the main thoroughfares, especially Market Place and Bridge Street, is of a Georgian town.

The Angel Inn and Posting House is typical of the coaching era with two bow windows and an arched entrance to the yard behind. Nearby are a number of buildings with attractive cast-iron first-floor balconies. From here Bridge Street leads to the largely medieval bridge across the Avon. Notable buildings include Barclays Bank (late eighteenth-century) with an elaborate doorway, Bedford House (Regency period) with a cast-iron balcony, and Perrott House (about 1760).

There are very pleasant riverside walks from the town centre car park and from the old bridge, which has been developed as a picnic site. Beyond the bridge are the village of Wick (page 39) and the gardens of the College of Horticulture. An extensive parkland area lies west of the abbey.

Abbey Church of the Holy Cross with St Eadburga, page 65; **Pershore Bridge Picnic Site**, page 49; **Pershore College of Horticulture**, page 78.

In the locality: Eckington Bridge Picnic Site, page 49; and churches at Besford, page 56; Croome d'Abitot, page 57; Great Comberton, page 60; Little Comberton, page 64; and Pirton, page 66.

Pirton
Church of St Peter, page 66.

Redditch

The town centre is a mixture of nineteenth-century buildings and modern architecture which has arisen because Redditch and its neighbouring communities were incorporated as an overspill town for the West Midlands. The parish church of St Stephen is nineteenth-century and is surrounded by a pleasant area of gardens and pedestrianised streets. Inside, it is a lofty, light building with painted barrel ceilings in the nave and aisles and a vaulted chancel. Among the points of interest are two Kemp windows in the south aisle and an unusual and striking Belgian window dedicated to Henry and Catherine Milward (1880). He was a prominent local needlemaker, a reminder of the time when Redditch was the needlemaking capital of the world. Near the church, the main shopping area has been completely refurbished as the Kingfisher Centre with a centrepiece of fountains and palm trees in a controlled environment.

Arrow Valley Lake and Country Park, page 45; **Bordesley Abbey Visitor Centre**, page 90; **Forge Mill Needle Museum**, page 90.

In the locality: Tardebigge church, page 69; Tardebigge Locks and Wharf, page 97.

Ripple

The village is grouped around a diminutive square with an ancient cross-shaft and a row of almshouses renovated in 1701. The huge church of St Mary dominates the village with its lofty central tower resting on massive pillars. The east window is particularly striking and the fifteenth-century misericords in the chancel depict the Labours of the Seasons. Beside the church is the impressive rectory of 1726.

Rock

Church of St Peter and St Paul, page 66.

Rous Lench

The immaculately maintained green, shaded by large trees, forms the centrepiece of this attractive small village. Many of the surrounding buildings are Victorian in timber and brick styles of the sixteenth and seventeenth centuries. The school of 1864 is a typical mixture of tall Gothic windows and timber work. Next to it is a roofed seat and across the green is the ornate postbox done up as a small house, complementary to those at nearby Abbots Morton and Radford (page 12).

Near the green is the church of St Peter in a churchyard of large yew trees. The south doorway is Norman with a blank tympanum but this is compensated for by the well-preserved figure of Christ in a niche above the arch. The outstanding feature inside is the 1885 chapel with its monuments to the Rous family. The north aisle has a Romanesque apse, also of 1885. In the chancel is a set of intricately carved chairs and in the nave a long oil painting of Jesus in the house of Simon the Pharisee.

Behind laurel bushes can be seen the moated site of a former castle and across the park is the timber-framed façade, mostly nineteenth-century, of Rous Lench Court. The road to Church Lench passes the Court, with its tall Italianate tower in the gardens.

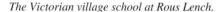

The Victorian village school at Rous Lench.

Salwarpe
Church of St Michael, page 67.

Shatterford
Koi Water Gardens, page 77.

Shelsley Beauchamp
Church of All Saints, page 67.

Shelsley Walsh
Near the church is the finely proportioned sixteenth-century Court House, formerly the seat of the Walsh family. Following the failure of the Gunpowder Plot (1605), Sir Richard Walsh, then High Sheriff, helped to arrest the perpetrators at Holbeach House near Stourbridge, at that time in Worcestershire.
Church of St Andrew, page 67.

Shrawley
Church of St Mary, page 68.

Spetchley
Church of All Saints, page 68; Spetchley Park, page 78.

Stock Green
White Cottage Garden, page 79.

Stockton on Teme
Church of St Andrew, page 68.

Stoke Prior
Church of St Nicholas, page 68; Stoke Wharf, page 97; Stoke Works, page 97.

Stone
Church of St Mary, page 69; Stone House Cottage Garden, page 79.

Stourport-on-Severn
Stourport has the distinction of being the only town in England created as a direct result of the canal era. James Brindley came to Worcestershire in 1765 and planned the Staffordshire & Worcestershire Canal to link the Severn with the Trent. His first proposal, to build the western terminus at Bewdley, having been rejected, Brindley settled on the unbuilt area at the confluence of the Stour and Severn. Here, in the space of only a few years in the 1770s, a Georgian town of dignity and charm grew up around the canal basin that linked the two rivers.

A period of great prosperity began, with Stourport second only to Birmingham as an inland port. Foundries for iron and brass, boatbuilding and carpet-making industries were established but with the coming of the railways the canal basins ceased to be the focal point for goods transport.

Today the legacy of that boom period is an almost wholly preserved Georgian inland port and town core. It is now a major centre for the inland waterways leisure-boat industry and a source of delight for all visitors interested in the industrial past and the history of transport.

Stourport has something for most visitors: riverside gardens and walks; the canal basins and locks; boat trips and boats for hire on the river; and a permanent riverside funfair. Particularly in the holiday season, the town has the atmosphere of an inland resort. There are opportunities for virtually unlimited walking along either bank of the river Severn and along the canal towpath towards Kidderminster.

Stourport Basins, page 95.

In the locality: Astley Vineyards, page 100; Hartlebury Castle State Rooms, page 76; Hereford and Worcester County Museum, page 87; Leapgate Country Park, page 46; and churches at Astley, page 55; Shrawley, page 68; and Wilden, page 70.

Tardebigge
Church of St Bartholomew, page 69; Tardebigge Locks and Wharf, page 97.

Tenbury Wells
An ancient market town in the Teme valley, Tenbury added 'Wells' to its name when it enjoyed a brief period of popularity as a spa in the nineteenth century, following the discovery of saline springs in 1839. Today Tenbury continues its role as a small market centre for the neighbouring valley and hillside villages and is noted for having England's largest specialist market days for holly and mistletoe in early December.

At the north of Teme Street, the town's main thoroughfare, is a medieval bridge lead-

Tenbury Wells: the Royal Oak in Market Street.

ing across to Shropshire. A walk south along Teme Street reveals a variety of timber-framed and brick-built buildings, many of them still unmarred by modern shop frontages.

Where Teme Street joins Market Street there is a smaller bridge across the turbulent Kyre Brook, hurrying to its nearby confluence with the Teme. Here, behind the Crow Inn and on the bank of the brook, lies the extraordinary semi-derelict former pump room of the spa, built in 1862. A structure of rusting iron and decaying timber, it is so tasteless and ugly as to be quite fascinating. A succession of restoration proposals have so far failed to come to fruition.

Along Market Street is Tenbury's most impressive building, the three-storeyed, ornately timbered Royal Oak, a reminder of the days when the town was an important staging post on the London to North Wales route. Further on is the pleasant Round Market built in 1811, with church-like windows all round and a two-stage roof.

From here Church Street leads to St Mary's church standing on the bank of the Teme. Church and churchyard are neat and tidy: the Victorians did a characteristically thorough restoration job in 1865. Only the tower shows signs of weathering: it is late Norman with a parapet added in the seventeenth century.

The interior offers more interest, particularly in the gallery, which spans the whole width of nave and both aisles at the west end, supported on slender iron columns. A wooden staircase leads up from the gallery to the bellchamber in the tower. Other points of interest are the fine alabaster monument to the Archers (1581), the pulpit with its stone figures of saints and some good windows in the east and south walls of the chancel.

Tenbury Museum, page 36.

In the locality: Burford House Gardens, page 72; Kyre Park, page 77.

Tibberton

Tibberton Bridge, page 97.

Upper Arley

This is one of Worcestershire's most delightful villages, located in the extreme north-western corner of the county. It is the first Worcestershire village on the river Severn as it flows southwards out of Shropshire, set in a steep-sided valley.

Upper Arley's attractions lie on both sides of the Severn, linked by a footbridge but no road bridge. On the east bank is the main part of the village with the church; on the west bank are the village inn and the station for the Severn Valley Railway. There are car parks on the riverbank on both sides and walks along the river, including a section of the Worcestershire Way (page 48).

The church of St Peter has a delightful setting: it occupies an elevated site at the top end of the village street, giving extensive views across the valley. The churchyard is well maintained, surrounded by a yew hedge and magnificent specimen conifers. There is a car park at the start of the curving drive to the church and the churchyard entrance crosses the line of a ha-ha.

The church interior has a number of interesting features. The east window, tall with five lights, is by Kempe and was installed in 1887 when the chancel was largely rebuilt. On the south wall is a roundel commemorating Captain Robert Woodward, who was killed in action in 1915.

Two arches separate the chancel from All Souls' Chapel. Under one arch is the tomb chest of a knight, generally thought to be Sir Walter de Belun, who was accidentally killed in a tournament on his wedding day. The east window of the chapel is of 1886, depicting scenes from the life of Jesus, and the curved rails separating the chapel from the north aisle date from Queen Anne's reign. The north-aisle windows have good coats of arms at the apexes.

The nave roof is timbered and, above the chancel arch, incorporates the old rood-loft beam, which is painted. The south wall of the nave has four monumental tablets; the best, nearest the door, is to Sir Henry Lyttleton, who died in 1693.

The village has a number of rather grandiose nineteenth-century buildings in the street leading down from the church. Along the river front are much more attractive brick-built cottages and a tea garden. From here the pedestrian bridge leads across to the inn and station.

Severn Valley Railway, page 101.

Upton upon Severn

This delightful and lovely unspoilt riverside town has much to offer the visitor. Its period of greatest significance and prosperity was the latter half of the eighteenth century, when the Severn was crowded with traffic. Being one of the few bridging points on the river, Upton was also an important staging point for road passengers, as its substantial inns testify. Before this, the town figured briefly in two Civil War engagements: in 1643 the Royalist

The Pepperpot at Upton upon Severn houses the Heritage Centre and the tourist information centre.

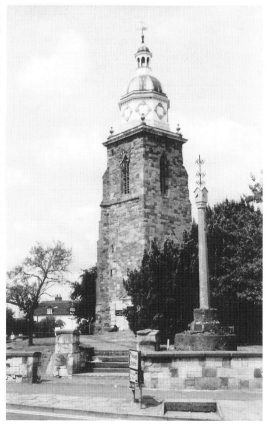

occupiers rebuffed an attack, and in 1651 the tables were turned when Scots supporters of Charles II were routed and driven back towards Worcester for their final defeat at the battle of Worcester.

Upton is a long narrow town, its development to the east and west being prohibited by the Severn's propensity towards spectacular flooding. There are parking areas at the northern end by the river and further south opposite the church.

The bridge makes a good starting point for an exploration of the town. Immediately beside it is Upton's unmistakeable landmark, the great tower of the medieval church, around 1300, surmounted by the extraordinary cupola of 1770, by Keek, who also designed the original Worcester Royal Infirmary. This is all that remains: the rest was demolished in 1937, its site now marked by a pleasant garden and the Heritage and Information Centre. There is also a bust to commemorate Admiral Sir William Tennant, a former Lord Lieutenant of Worcestershire, who played a prominent part in both the Dunkirk evacuation and the Normandy landings.

Downstream from the bridge are the quays where pleasure boats now moor. Along Waterside are Waterside House and the Malthouse, the two most substantial Georgian houses in the town. Also here is a Dutch gable-ended building, used as a barracks and stabling during the Civil War. On the opposite bank can be seen the entrance to Upton marina, which accommodates scores of the pleasure cruisers which ply the Severn in summer.

Returning towards the bridge, the High Street runs south towards the prominent slender spire of the church of St Peter and St Paul. Both sides of the street are full of delightful buildings, Georgian formality mixing happily with older timber-framed constructions. Most prominent is the White Lion, with its porch projecting across the pavement and surmounted by a large lion. It is widely claimed that Henry Fielding used this inn as the setting for some of the escapades of his hero Tom Jones.

The church, at the southern end of the street, is wholly Victorian of 1879, but its interior is more interesting than many of its kind. The most prominent feature is the huge metal abstract sculpture suspended above the nave altar, about which visitors must form their own opinions.

Less startling is a superb west window, a monument (1905) to a lord of the manor, G. E. Martin. There are also pleasant windows in the aisles and east wall of the chancel. The nave roof has impressive timbers while the chancel is barrel-vaulted with faded paintings.

Upton Heritage Centre, page 91.

In the locality: Hill Croome Dovecote, page 52; Dunstall Castle Folly, page 100.

Wichenford

Wichenford Dovecote, page 54.

Wick

Wick is a model village, immaculately maintained in a delightful setting, its single street running along the base of a park-like hillside. The little church of St Bartholomew is basically Norman with Victorian restoration. The chancel has a barrel roof and some enjoyable windows; it is separated from the nave by a good nineteenth-century screen. The nave has a good south window and there is a bishop's window in the north aisle. Two carved heads and the intricate apex of the preaching cross are on display.

The cross stands in a field adjacent to the beautifully tended churchyard. The apex was blown down in 1984 and is kept inside now. The lychgate has a good carved bargeboard and opposite is the village's most impressive building, Wick Manor. Looking like an elaborate Jacobean timber-framed house, it actually dates from 1923 but is nonetheless picturesque. Further along the street to the north is a cruck-frame cottage.

In the locality: Pershore College of Horticulture, page 78.

Wilden

Church of all Saints, page 70.

Wolverley

A village of quite extraordinary character and atmosphere, Wolverley is located in the Stour

The remains of rock houses in the red sandstone at Wolverley.

valley, just north of Kidderminster. Here the western side of the valley is bounded by a sheer cliff of Old Red Sandstone and at the foot of the cliff lies Wolverley.

The best viewpoint from which to take in the layout of the village is slightly up the sloping main street, well back from the cliff. The church then comes into view perched on the top and dominating the village with its massive red-brick bulk.

On the left is the unusual Sebright School, founded in the seventeenth century by William Sebright; the buildings here are of the 1820s. The main school hall is an imposing affair which is approached by two sets of steps leading up to a central terrace. The double doorway is flanked by two very tall three-light windows of church proportions. There are slender turrets on each side of the building and a coat of arms with the date 1620, when the school was founded, surmounts the façade. Two lower buildings adjoin this structure and two further ones project at an angle, to make the whole range face the village street.

Down the street towards the cliff a terrace of Gothick cottages faces the village inn and shops. Two bridges cross a small stream. The one into the large inn car park leads to caves in the base of the cliff: its face shows innumerable recesses which once took the roof beams of double-storey houses built on to the cliff face. Finds indicate that these caves and those at other sites in the locality were inhabited as long ago as neolithic times.

Crossing the other bridge, the road winds up through the most picturesque part of the village. Here the cottages are all white-painted, their delightful gardens crammed in between the stream and the cliff base. One cottage actually grows out of the rock, which has been painted white to match. The narrow little street is overhung by the sheer cliff in places.

At the top of the street a flight of steps leads up to the churchyard. The church of St John the Baptist is of 1722, hardly pretty but certainly impressive, with a massive tower and nave all battlemented. Inside is a feeling of space and light and two of the large windows of the chancel are by Morris & Company. (1899).

The unusually large number of monuments provide a lot of interest, ranging from an early figure of a fourteenth-century knight, with his legs missing, through a series of eighteenth-century wall tablets to the more complicated monuments of the nineteenth century.

In the locality: Kingsford Country Park, page 46.

Worcester

Worcester is one of England's major cathedral cities and has a long, proud and at times turbulent history. The site of the original settlement was a well-drained ridge of gravels, close to the river Severn but above its flood levels, a site with natural marshland defences.

Although so far upstream, the river here was tidal, with an average tide of 6 feet (2 metres), and could be forded twice daily at low tide, except in times of flood. This was the lowest point of the Severn that could be reliably forded. The Severn was the major transport artery for these western counties but, like all English rivers, it was unreliable and unpredictable.

Relics of pre-Roman occupation are scarce, limited to scattered flints and implements and indications of earthworks on the southern extremity of the ridge, probably of iron age date.

A Roman fort, with progressively stronger fortifications, was established with a northern suburb which developed an important iron-smelting function in the later stages of Roman occupation. Following the collapse of Roman rule, a see was established and a cathedral built in 680. Little is known of the Saxon centuries, when, it is thought, a fortified borough was established.

Shortly after the Norman Conquest a castle, first wooden, then stone, was built to guard the ford. A rebuilding of the cathedral was begun by Bishop Wulfstan in 1084. The first recognisable form of the modern name appeared in Domesday (1086): the settlement was recorded as 'Wirecestre'.

By the mid twelfth century medieval Worcester was well-fortified with a substantial stone wall and nine gates and the city gained its first royal charter from Richard I in 1189. The cathedral, with its extensive mon-

astic settlement, dominated the city and there were also houses of Greyfriars and Blackfriars. All these religious communities were swept away by Henry VIII, who refounded the cathedral without a priory but with a dean and canons and established the King's School.

In the 1640s Worcester was generally Royalist, like most cathedral cities, and earned its title of 'The Faithful City'. A period of steadily increasing prosperity followed the restoration of the monarchy in 1660 and in 1690 the first edition of a Worcester-based newspaper appeared. This subsequently became *Berrows Worcester Journal* and now has the distinction of being the world's oldest surviving newspaper.

Georgian Worcester was highly praised by travellers for its clean elegant streets and buildings and businesslike atmosphere. Porcelain manufacturing began in 1751 (see page 107) and glovemaking had become the city's dominant industry by the close of the eighteenth century.

Edgar Tower gateway at College Green, Worcester.

In 1815 the Worcester & Birmingham Canal was completed and the city became a strategic location for a wide range of engineering and other metal-based industries: the foundations of today's broadly based economy had been laid. Today Worcester has the air of a dynamic purposeful city, looking to the future but proud of its long past, and careful to preserve its best elements.

To see all that central Worcester has to offer the visitor needs at least a full day. The walks described here take in the city's major attractions and main historic thoroughfares.

Walk 1: the historic city

Start at the Guildhall in High Street, which also houses the tourist information centre. On leaving the Guildhall, turn right along the pedestrianised High Street to the statue of Edward Elgar (page 103) looking across to his beloved cathedral. Cross the road to the South African War Memorial, then turn right, following the semicircular College Yard of late Georgian houses round to the ornate north porch of the cathedral (see page 70 for a description of a walk round the cathedral and College Green).

Leave College Green by Edgar Tower gateway and bear right into Severn Street, where the Royal Worcester Porcelain factory and museum are seen on the opposite side of the street. On leaving Royal Worcester, turn right, then right again along the short King Street to emerge at Sidbury, a busy dual carriageway. Opposite is the Commandery Civil War Centre.

From the Commandery turn right along Sidbury. Immediately beside the building the road crosses the canal and a plaque on the bridge parapet records this as being the site of Sidbury Gate, where wholesale slaughter of Scots Royalist troops took place in the battle of Worcester (1651).

Beyond the ring road bear right along Friar Street, one of the city's medieval thoroughfares, lined with interesting specialist shops and good examples of timber-framed buildings. Here, on the right, is Greyfriars, one of Worcester's best timber-framed buildings, now in the care of the National Trust. On the left is Tudor House Museum.

Continue straight ahead, across a small junction, to New Street, for more medieval buildings. Towards the end of the street, on the right, is King Charles II House, now well

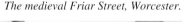

The medieval Friar Street, Worcester.

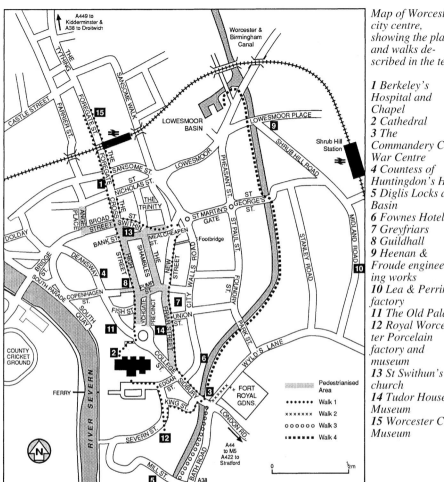

Map of Worcester
city centre,
showing the places
and walks de-
scribed in the text:

1 *Berkeley's
Hospital and
Chapel*
2 *Cathedral*
3 *The
Commandery Civil
War Centre*
4 *Countess of
Huntingdon's Hall*
5 *Diglis Locks and
Basin*
6 *Fownes Hotel*
7 *Greyfriars*
8 *Guildhall*
9 *Heenan &
Froude engineer-
ing works*
10 *Lea & Perrins
factory*
11 *The Old Palace*
12 *Royal Worces-
ter Porcelain
factory and
museum*
13 *St Swithun's
church*
14 *Tudor House
Museum*
15 *Worcester City
Museum*

restored as a restaurant. From here, Charles II escaped Cromwell's men after the disastrous battle of Worcester. This house was also the birthplace of Judge William Berkeley in 1584 and there is a dungeon in which he allegedly kept the prisoners awaiting trial.

A few yards further on the street opens out and ends. Here turn left and walk along pedestrianised Mealcheapen Street. Before doing so, however, look sharp right at another fine timber-framed building with its Georgian bow-fronted shop windows still in use. Mealcheapen Street leads into St Swithin Street, at the end of which turn right in Worcester's main thoroughfare, The Cross. Ahead of you is the ornate cast-iron railway bridge and, a short walk beyond the bridge on the right, is Worcester City Museum and Art Gallery.

On leaving the museum, turn left back towards the city centre. Passing under the railway bridge, cross the road, pass the entrance to Shaw Street and on your right are the entrance gates to Berkeley's Hospital, a quadrangle of Queen Anne almshouses and chapel, one of Worcester's architectural gems. The Warden's house is on the left inside the gate. Now turn right along the pedestrianised High Street to your starting point at the Guildhall.

Walk 2: a Civil War walk to Fort Royal Gardens

Fort Royal was a star-shaped earthwork constructed by Royalist defenders of Worcester during the Civil War, around 1650. The southern part of the city, around the cathedral, had been bombarded by cannon fire from this hill by the Parliamentarian forces in 1643 and 1646.

The Commandery Civil War Centre makes a good starting point for the short walk to Fort Royal. From the Commandery, turn left along Sidbury, then first left into Wylde's Lane. A short distance along on the right are two entrances to Fort Royal Gardens. Paths lead steeply upwards to the summit, where some of the outlines of the earthworks can still be discerned.

In pleasant weather this is a delightful spot to rest and admire the excellent panorama across the rooftops to the cathedral. The line of nineteenth-century warehouses and the Worcester Porcelain works along the canal can be picked out in the foreground, including the well-restored former Fownes glove factory, now a luxury hotel.

Walk 3: the canal towards Diglis Basin

The Commandery is also a convenient starting point for two canalside walks along the Worcester & Birmingham Canal. Whether in urban or rural surroundings, canal towpaths always provide a refreshing and revealing alternative to following highways.

From the Commandery Quay, turn left under the Sidbury bridge. The canal flows between a variety of industrial premises including Worcester Porcelain. To the right are frequent views of the cathedral tower and to the left the large houses along Bath Road. Diglis Basin has a delightful collection of decorated narrowboats, a basin master's house and two locks leading down to the Severn. A little further downstream is the massive double lock where the canal has its junction with the Severn.

Walk 4: the canal towards Lowesmoor Basin

From the Commandery Quay, turn right and follow the towpath past industrial premises, a lock and two bridges until approaching the railway viaduct. Here the entrance to Lowesmoor Basin is on the left and a footpath runs beside the basin back into the city centre.

Walks 3 and 4 can be combined with a walk along the frontage of the city with the river Severn to form a circular walk around the historic centre of Worcester.

Other walks in the city centre

Recent commercial developments have been wholly beneficial to residents and visitors alike. Apart from providing a wide variety of shopping and other amenities, they have restored and revitalised many run-down backland areas and alleys and given a new lease of life to a number of important buildings, especially the Countess of Huntingdon's Hall in the Crowngate Development.

A Crowngate Heritage Trail has been marked out with informative display boards and a leaflet is available from the tourist information centre. Other areas in the city worth exploring are Reindeer Court, Hopmarket Yard and Crown Passage.

Berkeley's Hospital and Chapel, page 72; **the Commandery Civil War Centre**, page 91; **Countess of Huntingdon's Hall**, page 72; **Diglis Locks and Basin**, page 97; **Fownes Hotel**, page 98; **the Greyfriars**, page 73; **Heenan & Froude engineering works**, page 99; **Lea & Perrins factory**, page 99; **the Old Palace**, page 78; **Royal Worcester Porcelain and Museum of Worcester Porcelain**, page 91; **St Swithun's church**, page 71; **Tudor House Museum**, page 92; **Worcester Cathedral**, page 70; **Worcester City Museum, Art Gallery and Library**, page 94; **Worcester Guildhall**, page 80.

In the locality: Bennetts's Farm Park, page 100; Elgar Birthplace Museum, page 88; Hawford Dovecote, page 52; Leigh Court Barn, page 52; Spetchley Park, page 78; Worcester Woods Country Park, page 47; and churches at Alfrick, page 55; Cotheridge, page 57; Croome d'Abitot, page 57; Crowle, page 58; Himbleton, page 62; Huddington, page 63; Leigh, page 64; Spetchley, page 68; and Warndon, page 69.

3
The countryside

Access to the countryside should present few problems in Worcestershire. The footpath network has received much attention in recent years: most villages have signposts leading off into the surrounding countryside. The main rivers and the canals have towing paths leading along their banks; there are a number of country parks, particularly in the north of the county, and three long-distance paths which can be tackled in sections, wherever they cross a public road. Malvern Hills are unique in having their own protection, the Malvern Hills Conservators, England's pioneering preservation trust.

Country parks

Worcestershire's country parks are concentrated in the north of the county, to cater for the larger urban areas and the West Midlands conurbation which reaches to the county's northern boundary. Leaflets describing the parks' attractions, facilities and walks are available in the tourist information and visitor centres.

Arrow Valley Lake and Country Park, Redditch. Telephone (Warden): 01527 68337. Off A4023. Car park at OS 150:SP 065678.

Within the built-up area of Redditch, this is an attractive and extensive 800 acre (340 hectare) park and lake created by damming the river Arrow. Facilities include picnic areas, fishing and boating.

Blackstone Meadows Country Park (OS 138: SO 790742), 1 mile (2 km) south of Bewdley on B4194 (OS 138: SO 790742). Hereford and Worcester County Council.

A car park and picnic area give access to pleasant walks beside the river Severn both upstream to Bewdley and downstream towards Ribbesford Wood (Forestry Commission).

Broadway Tower Country Park, Fish Hill, Broadway WR12 7LB (OS 150: SP 113360). Telephone: 01386 852390. Off A44 at the top of Fish Hill, 2 miles (3 km) east of Broadway. *Open: April to October, daily.*

The park occupies a spectacular location on the crest of the Cotswold escarpment overlooking Broadway, the only part of Worces-

tershire to be actually on the Cotswolds. Broadway Tower, with its superb views over Worcestershire and twelve neighbouring counties, was built as a folly in 1789 by the sixth Earl of Coventry. The tower has three turrets, battlemented in the medieval style popular at the time. There are three floors, which house exhibitions on the park landscape, sheep rearing and the Pre-Raphaelite Brotherhood. In the mid nineteenth century this was a holiday retreat for William Morris and Edward Burne-Jones. From here, Morris wrote a letter in 1876 which led to the formation of the Society for the Protection of Ancient Buildings.

The park surrounding the tower has a highland air, with long-coated cattle and red deer grazing peacefully on the springy turf. There are a number of waymarked walks, including part of the Cotswold Way long-distance footpath, and a range of other facilities: refreshment bar, picnic areas, barbecue and adventure playground. The Cotswold Way leads down the hill to Broadway, and a footpath runs along the ridge to nearby Fish Hill picnic area and nature trail.

Clent Hills Country Park, off A456 8 miles (12 km) north-east of Kidderminster. Visitor centre at OS 139: SO 939809. There is also a car park at SO 927798 approached through the village of Clent. National Trust.

A delightful upland area with a variety of woodlands, heathland and farmland, the country park extends to over 500 acres (210 hectares). There are numerous waymarked trails, including two with easy access. Walton Hill

Four Stones on the summit of the Clent Hills.

at 1035 feet (318 metres) is the second highest point in Worcestershire and provides superb all-round views. Clent Grove is an adjoining National Trust area looking down over Hagley Park. Hereford and Worcester County Council has a visitor centre, car park and picnic area at OS 139: SO 939809.

Kingsford Country Park, 4 miles (6 km) north of Kidderminster on the county boundary. Car park at OS 138: SO 823821. Hereford and Worcester County Council.

Here are 200 acres (85 hectares) of open heathland and coniferous plantations rising up from Kingsford village. There are a number of waymarked paths and extensive views. The open land extends northwards into Kinver Edge (Staffordshire) with a further 400 acres (170 hectares) culminating in the elevated viewpoint of Holy Austin Rock. The Worcestershire Way, the North Worcestershire Path and the Staffordshire Way all start here (see entries later in this chapter).

Leapgate Country Park, 1 mile (2 km) east of Stourport on B4193. Car park at OS 138: SO 825714. Hereford and Worcester County Council.

This is Hartlebury Common; the open heathland which includes a pool and coppiced woodland is regarded as one of Worcestershire's most important nature reserves, noted for wild plants, moths and butterflies. A disused railway track provides a level bridleway and there are waymarked walks and a picnic area.

Lickey Hills Country Park, Warren Lane, Rednal, Birmingham B45 8ER. Telephone: 0121-447 7106. 5 miles (8 km) north-east of Bromsgrove on B4096, then along a minor road through the village of Lickey to car park at OS 139: SO 988760. There is also a visitor centre at SO 999753. Bromsgrove District Council.

Beacon Hill rises beside the car park and provides an excellent north-facing viewpoint. There is a varied landscape of ornamental gardens, heathland and bog, as well as extensive hill areas of mixed deciduous and coniferous woodland. The visitor centre on Warren Lane, owned and managed by Birmingham City Council, provides information, refreshments and toilets. The rangers provide an educational service, guided walks and activities.

The Malvern Hills

One might easily envy anyone who has yet to see the Malvern Hills: the first sight of their dramatic outline must surely rank as one of the major highlights of any holiday. From all over the Worcestershire plain to the east, the familiar outline of the hills forms the western horizon of the county. Close up, the drama increases as the hills rear steeply up from the lowlands, with Great Malvern and its satellite villages lined along the lower slopes.

The Malverns are everyone's hills: easily accessible and providing suitable terrain for every kind of walking, from a stroll with the dog to a strenuous hike along their whole 9 mile (12 km) length. Good roads and several car parks encircle the northern part of the range, but the southern hills are rather less accessible and therefore less heavily visited.

The highest point is Worcestershire Beacon (1380 feet, 425 metres), which, together with neighbouring North Hill (1295 feet, 398 metres), rises directly from the upper streets of Great Malvern. Further south, Herefordshire Beacon is crowned with a major iron age camp and then come the much less frequented Midsummer Hill, with another iron age camp, Hollybush Hill and, right on the Gloucestershire border, Chase End Hill.

Because of their narrow ridge-like character, especially at the northern end, the Malverns offer spectacular and contrasting views in all directions, particularly between the Worcestershire plain and, to the west, the rolling hills of Herefordshire, leading the eye across to the distant Welsh border.

Walking maps are readily available from the Great Malvern tourist information centre and some bookshops, and the OS Landranger sheet 150 is useful for planning motoring tours and access.

Seckley Wood and Hawkbatch Valleys (OS 138: SO 763778). On B4194 3 miles (5 km) north-west of Bewdley.

There are waymarked walks through delightful woodland and superb views from the spectacular sandstone cliff down to the river Severn, Trimpley Reservoir and perhaps a steam train making its way along the Severn Valley line.

Waseley Hill Country Park, 5 miles (8 km) north of Bromsgrove. Minor road leads off B4551 and over M5 motorway. Car park at OS 139: SO 971782. Visitor centre and refreshments. Secondary car park off A38 on the south side of the hill at SO 977769, adjacent to National Trust area. Hereford and Worcester County Council.

This is largely open hillside, with some woodland areas, rising to over 900 feet (280 metres). The contrasting views are spectacular: the M5 curves round the base of the hill to plunge northwards into the Black Country; north-east is Birmingham city centre and west lies the farmland of north Worcestershire, stretching across to the river Severn. There is a toposcope on the summit of Windmill Hill.

Worcester Woods Country Park, on the eastern edge of Worcester, on A422, approached through main entrance to County Hall at OS 150: SO 876540. Hereford and Worcester County Council. Telephone: 01905 766493.
Open: daily.

Nunnery Wood is 150 acres (52 hectares) of ancient woodlands with waymarked paths and an orienteering course. There is a good Countryside Centre with informative displays, a shop and refreshments.

The Wyre Forest Visitor Centre (OS 138: SO 751741). On A456 3 miles (5 km) west of Bewdley. Forestry Commission. Telephone: 01299 266302.
Open daily.

Here there are forest interpretation displays, information, refreshments, car park, picnic area and a number of waymarked circular walks.

Wyre Forest lies north-west of Bewdley and extends into neighbouring Shropshire. It occupies upland west of the river Severn and is generally regarded as one of the best surviving native woodlands in Britain. It covers 6000 acres (2400 hectares), half of which belongs to the Forestry Commission. There are a number of nature reserves in the remaining area.

Inevitably, large areas have been given over to conifer plantations but there remain

The Countryside Centre at Worcester Woods Country Park.

substantial areas of mixed broadleaf, of which the oak woods are the chief glory. The forest is noted for its rich wildlife: plants, birds and insects. There are two recommended access points where car parks and picnic facilities are provided.

Long-distance paths

These paths give access to a wide variety of scenery. Details are available from tourist information centres (chapter 13) or the visitor centres at the country parks.

North Worcestershire Path (OS 139).

The path runs 26 miles (42 km) along the county's northern boundary from Kingsford Country Park to Major's Green (OS 139: SP 103782). It passes through three other country parks (Clent Hills, Waseley Hill and Lickey Hills) and skirts the deer park of Hagley Hall. It also passes Upper Bittell Reservoir (OS 139: SP 020755), now a nationally important waterfowl habitat, originally created to provide water for Tardebigge Locks, and Forhill Picnic Site (OS 139: SP 055757).

Worcestershire Way (OS 138 and 150).

This 40 mile (64 km) path follows the county's western boundary and also starts in Kingsford Country Park, at Vales Rock (OS 138: SO 825822). This is also the southern end of the Staffordshire Way, which leads north for 92 miles (147 km). The Worcestershire Way leaflet shows the path divided into ten self-contained sections, some including loop walks. A wide variety of walking terrain includes Shatterford Lakes, the Severn valley, Abberley Hills, the Teme valley and the Malvern Hills. A southern extension along the Malverns to the Gloucestershire border is planned.

Wychavon Way (OS 150).

This 40 mile (64 km) path crosses varied and attractive countryside in central and south Worcestershire. The southernmost 5 miles (8 km) are in Gloucestershire, ending at Winchcombe, where it links with the Cotswold Way footpath. The northern starting point is at Holt Fleet (OS 150: SO 825634) on the Severn. The route includes Ombersley, Droitwich, a stretch of the Worcester & Birmingham Canal, the river Avon, the Vale of Evesham and Bredon Hill. It crosses innumerable roads and there are therefore many opportunities for visitors to sample sections in areas which particularly appeal to them. The southern starting point is on the A435 at OS 150: SP 001366.

Walks and forest trails

Avon Valley

There are two riverside car parks with picnic sites. Both are the starting points for attractive river and meadowland walks.

Eckington Bridge picnic site (OS 150: SO 922423); on B4080 4 miles (6 km) south-west of Pershore. The bridge is fifteenth- or sixteenth-century, with prominent cutwaters on both sides.

Pershore Bridge picnic site (OS 150: SO 953452); off A44 on southern edge of Pershore. This bridge is of similar age, or perhaps slightly earlier. One arch was destroyed in the Civil War, by Royalists fleeing from Worcester in 1651.

Bredon Hill (OS 150).

The hill and its slopes cover a fairly extensive area of about 12 square miles (30 square km) and there are innumerable footpaths setting off from the villages which surround the hill. Wychavon Way crosses the north-west corner of the hill from Elmley Castle to Ashton under Hill. Walking guides are available from Evesham and Pershore tourist offices and some local shops.

Fish Hill (OS 150: SP 120370). Off A44 east of Broadway.

Located on the crest of the Cotswold escarpment with extensive views across the Vale of Evesham, this area has invigorating walking at any time of the year. There is a large car-parking area and picnic site. The Cotswold Way long-distance footpath runs along here. There is a toposcope at the summit of Fish Hill.

Habberley Valley (OS 138: SO 808771). Off B4190 2 miles (3 km) north-west of Kidderminster. Ranger Centre: telephone 01562 827800.

The valley contains extensive broadleaf woodland punctuated by dramatic outcrops of sandstone crags and cliffs. Oak, birch and mountain ash are interspersed with more open areas of heather and bracken. The valley floor provides a habitat for slow-worms, adders and common lizards. The Ranger Centre is the starting point for two circular walks, north and south along the valley.

Salwarpe Valley Nature Trails (car park at OS 150: SO887634).

These trails circle an area on the western edge of Droitwich, between the canal and the river Salwarpe. The valley here is one of the few inland sites where salt water occurs. This provides conditions for several saltmarsh plants to grow. Despite being bounded by the busy bypass, there are several different habitats which support a varied wildlife: the river, the canal, hedgerows, grassland and damp valley-floor areas. There is a car park in Ombersley Way, which passes through the area.

The old bridge across the river Avon, from Pershore Bridge picnic site.

Nature reserves

Cleeve Prior Nature Reserve (OS 150: SP 079496). Just west of Cleeve Prior village along a bridleway. Worcestershire Nature Conservation Trust.
Open: at any time.

The western edge of Cleeve Hill drops steeply to the river Avon, which here forms the boundary between Worcestershire and Warwickshire. Visitors can walk on areas of limestone grassland and scrub and enjoy extensive views westward to Worcester and the Malvern Hills.

Devil's Spittleful and Rifle Range Nature Reserve, Kidderminster. Off A456 midway between Kidderminster and Bewdley. Access is along a track running along the boundary of the West Midlands Safari Park on the Kidderminster side; track leaves road at OS 138: SO 807759. Worcestershire Nature Conservation Trust.
Open: at any time.

This is one of the largest heathland areas in Worcestershire, covering some 150 acres (60 hectares).

Knapp and Papermill Nature Reserve, Alfrick (OS 150: SO 751522). 1 mile (2 km) south of Alfrick where Leigh Brook is crossed by a minor road. Park by bridge. Worcestershire Nature Conservation Trust. Telephone (general enquiries): 01905 754919.

Open: at any time.

There are 60 acres (24 hectares) of woodland, meadow, orchards, marsh and stream, with a nature trail marked out. Access is through Knapp House and there is a sales centre at the warden's house.

Ravenshill Woodland Nature Reserve, Alfrick (OS 150: SO 739539). 1 mile (2 km) north-west of Alfrick on minor road. Car park at entrance. Private ownership. Telephone (warden): 01886 21661.
Open: Easter to October. Other times by appointment.

There are two waymarked trails through this commercially managed woodland. On the opposite side of the road is a large pool which attracts waterfowl and herons. There is an information and sales centre and picnic area by the car park.

Windmill Hill Nature Reserve, Middle Littleton. Off B4510 5 miles (8 km) north-east of Evesham town centre. Access along bridleway leaving road at OS 150: SP 067471. Worcestershire Nature Conservation Trust.
Open: at any time.

This is an area of rich limestone grassland of about 15 acres (6 hectares) rising steeply on the east bank of the river Avon. It is a continuation of the feature found 2 miles (3 km) to the north at Cleeve Prior (see above). There is a marked nature trail and there are extensive views across the Avon valley and Severn lowlands.

4
Ancient sites and buildings

Bordesley Abbey, Needle Mill Lane, Riverside, Redditch B97 6RR. See page 90.

Bredon Barn, Bredon (OS 150: SO 919369). National Trust. Telephone (Regional Office): 01684 850051.
Open: April to November, Wednesdays, Thursdays, Saturdays and Sundays; in winter by appointment.

This great stone barn, with superb beams over its main storage area and two aisles, is 132 feet (40 metres) long. The two wagon entrances have porches, one of which has outside steps to an upper room, probably for a bailiff to record receipts. It is frequently referred to as a tithe barn but more probably it was a manorial barn, for storage of grain due to the lord of the manor. The building has a steeply pitched roof, with narrow slit and square openings in each end wall, and dates from the early fourteenth century. A visit can be combined with a walk around Bredon village.

British Camp, Malvern Hills. Car park on A449 at OS 150: SO 763404.

This is one of Britain's major pre-Roman settlements, occupying a dramatic site above a pass through the Malvern Hills. The site is elongated, with the successive rows of ramparts curving to fit the contours of the summit. The whole enclosed area is some 20 acres (8 hectares). Access is obtained by following a fairly steep path, stepped in places, from the car park. A medieval castle was built within the prehistoric ramparts but only the mound remains. 2 miles (3 km) south lies Midsummer Hill, another pre-Roman settlement.

Dormston Dovecote, Moat Farm, Dormston, near Inkberrow (OS 150: SO 984572).

Open: throughout the year during daylight hours.

This is a square timber-framed dovecote standing in front of the superb Moat Farmhouse; both date from 1663. The dovecote was restored by Avoncroft Museum of Historic Buildings, which now owns it. It has a tiled roof topped with a four-gabled lantern. All round the walls, halfway up, a ledge projects to stop rats running up and taking eggs. Dormston church (page 59) is nearby.

Evesham Abbey. See page 23.

Fleece Inn, Bretforton. National Trust. Telephone: 01386 831173.
Open: during normal licensed hours.

Located in the village square at Bretforton, the Fleece is one end of a good range of timber-framed buildings. Originally a medieval farmhouse, it was licensed in 1848 and has been very little altered.

The Fleece Inn, Bretforton.

Great Malvern Priory. See page 60.

Hartlebury Castle, Hartlebury, Kidderminster DY11 7XZ. See pages 76 and 87.

Hawford Dovecote, Hawford (OS 150: SO 846607). Off A449 4 miles (7 km) north of Worcester city centre. National Trust.
Open: April to October, daily except Good Friday.
This sixteenth-century square timber-framed dovecote with closely set timbers stands next to Hawford Grange. It has been well restored and contains remnants of trellis-work nest compartments.

Hill Croome Dovecote, Hill Croome (OS 150: SO 886404). 3 miles (5 km) east of Upton upon Severn.*Open: throughout the year during daylight hours.*
This interesting, possibly unique, square cruck-framed construction of the fifteenth century stands next to the church. It was dismantled and repaired at Avoncroft Museum, then re-erected on its original site.

Holt Castle, Holt (OS 150: SO 829627). 2 miles (3 km) west of Ombersley off A4133.
Not open to the public: visible from road outside Holt church.
Only a fourteenth-century four-storey tower remains of the original castle, which probably had three further towers. It stands in front of a fifteenth-century hall as part of the house. The two were joined in the early eighteenth century.

Kemerton Camp, Bredon Hill (OS 150: SO 957402).
Located on the crest of the northern slope of Bredon Hill, this pre-Roman settlement retains only part of its earthworks, which formerly enclosed an area of some 22 acres (9 hectares). The views to the north, across the Avon valley and Pershore, are extensive and exhilarating. Access is most convenient from Great Comberton: a footpath runs up the flank of the hill from the southern end of the village, beyond the church. It is, however, a fairly strenuous walk, rather than an afternoon stroll. Another footpath climbs up from Elmley Castle but is longer and no less strenuous. A footpath connects Elmley Castle with Great Comberton, running along the base of the slope. This completes a circular walk through delightful and varied countryside.

Leigh Court Barn, Leigh (OS 150: SO 784534). Off A4103 5 miles (8 km) west of Worcester. English Heritage. Telephone (regional office): 01743 761101.
Open: summer season, Thursday to Sunday.
This is a huge barn, the largest of its type in Britain, some 150 feet (46 metres) long by 35 feet (11 metres) wide, and of similar height. The main structure is of eleven massive pairs of cruck beams with the hipped roof shaped to fit their curve. There are two porched wagon doors, also of cruck construction. The barn was built in the fourteenth century for the abbey at Pershore. Nearby is Leigh church (page 64).

Little Malvern Priory. See page 64.

Hawford Dovecote.

The tithe barn at Middle Littleton belonged to Evesham Abbey.

Middle Littleton Tithe Barn, Middle Littleton (OS 150: SP 080470). Off B4085 4 miles (7 km) north-east of Evesham. National Trust. *Open: April to October, daily except Good Friday.*

Probably fourteenth-century, this barn belonged to Evesham Abbey and is built of stone with buttresses and superb timbers inside. It is 136 feet (42 metres) long and 32 feet (10 metres) wide. Only one of the two wagon entrance porches survives. The barn lies beside the church (page 65).

Midsummer Hill, Malvern Hills. Car park on A438 at OS 150: SO 759369.

Less dramatically located and less complex in structure than British Camp, this is nevertheless an impressive site with enjoyable and

The timber-framed Leigh Court Barn is the largest of its type in Britain.

Wichenford Dovecote.

extensive views. Excavations have indicated around five centuries of continuous pre-Roman occupation in about 250 buildings. Access is fairly gentle from the car park, past quarries, which give good exposures of the Malvern Precambrian rocks. The summit belongs to the National Trust.

Pershore Abbey. See page 65.

Wichenford Dovecote, Wichenford (OS 150: SO 787598). Along minor road off B4204 7 miles (11 km) north-west of Worcester. National Trust.
Open: April to October, daily except Good Friday.

This tall seventeenth-century timber-framed dovecote stands on a stone base and has a lantern on top.

5
Churches

In Worcestershire, as in all areas of Britain, some parishes feel compelled to keep their churches locked most of the time. This is obviously most likely in remote areas out of the main visitor season. Others are clearly determined to remain open and welcome visitors. Frequently there are notices indicating where keys are held locally. A few churches are in the care of the Redundant Churches Fund and this is indicated as RCF in the individual headings. Keys for these churches are also usually held locally.

Alfrick: St Mary Magdalene. (West of A4103, west of Worcester.)

Almost ruinous in the nineteenth century, this little church was well restored in 1885 and stands in a delightful elevated churchyard above the village green with its war memorial. Outside, the nave is topped with a small timber-framed bell turret and spire with chestnut shingles. Inside, the nave, which remains basically Norman, has impressive mid fifteenth-century roof timbers and interesting windows featuring Flemish motifs. The pulpit is Jacobean and the chancel screen contains some Tudor carving. The north transept contains items removed from nearby Lulsley church when it was closed in 1973. In the sanctuary is an example of modern craftsmanship: a hand-woven carpet made by local needlewomen in 1968. The Reverend Charles Dodgson (Lewis Carroll) preached here on one occasion when visiting his brother, who was curate in charge.

Astley: St Peter. (West of B4196, south-west of Stourport.)

Prominently sited on a hill, the tall tower is a local landmark. A good deal of Norman work survives, including a series of heads above the south porch, although those that have not been renewed are badly weathered. The Blount family tombs in the north chancel chapel are the chief point of interest; superbly preserved and painted, they provide a wealth of detail of knights' and ladies' costumes of the sixteenth century. On the north wall nearby are a number of interesting white marble monuments to the Winford family of the eighteenth and early nineteenth centuries.

In the churchyard is the white tomb of W. H. Havergall, rector here in the mid nineteenth century, and beside him lies his daughter, Frances Ridley Havergall, a prolific writer of hymns still sung today; 'Who is on the Lord's side?' is probably the best-known.

Beckford: St John the Baptist. (Off A435, south-west of Evesham.)

The fifteenth-century porch with its stone benches protects an intricate and entertaining Norman doorway – a foretaste of what is inside. The double row of zigzag carving and little details on the column heads are notable but it is the tympanum which commands most attention, featuring crudely carved animals with a cross and bird perched on one of its arms.

Inside, the vista is of a Norman nave looking through nave and chancel arches to the three-light east window. The nave windows span various architectural styles, the post-Norman one containing some good stained glass. The oak pews have intricately carved ends and there is a good fifteenth-century font in the centre of the nave. The north door, long since blocked up, frames a brass memorial to the fallen of the two world wars. From outside, it will be seen that it also has a tympanum; unprotected by a porch, it is badly weathered.

The tower arch contains more quaint carving on its north pillar: a centaur and two grotesque masks. Under the central tower there is a richly carved family pew opposite the organ. The chancel has a fine queen-post roof and four of the original lancet windows. The chancel screen incorporates portions of an older screen.

The village green and main street contain enjoyable buildings and on the outskirts of the village is Beckford Silk Printing Centre.

Besford: St Peter. (North of A4104, south-west of Pershore.)

Tucked away among farm buildings, this is one of Worcestershire's best-kept secrets, with its fourteenth-century timber-framed nave surmounted by a small turret housing two bells of around 1300. The porch is also of ancient timbers, probably fifteenth-century.

The interior is full of delights: the nave roof has magnificent timbers; the walls are panelled from old box pews; the pulpit is superbly carved and the west window is medieval. The rood loft is a rare survival, retaining its original painted fascia of rosettes and intertwined leaves and vines.

The chancel contains the Harewell tomb of Richard who died in 1576, aged fifteen. His recumbent alabaster effigy is backed by oak panelling while the tomb chest contains carvings of a hare, a child and armorials. The other notable monument, also of the Harewell family, is a triptych on the south wall of the nave. Three sons of the next generation also died young and this monument probably commemorates them. There is a further series of monuments and reliefs to the Sebright family, who succeeded the Harewells as lords of the manor in the seventeenth century.

Birtsmorton: St Peter and St Paul. (North of A438, west of Tewkesbury.)

Before entering the church the visitor's attention will inevitably be attracted by the picturesque Birtsmorton Court (not open, but see page 14). The church contains numerous monuments to the Nanfan family and an impressive memorial to Admiral William Caldwell of 1718: he reclines on a tomb-chest which depicts his flagship. The plaque is accompanied by nautical instruments and military trophies. See also the Norman font, the sixteenth-century carved pews and windows of the fourteenth and nineteenth centuries.

Bushley: St Peter. (North of A438, west of Tewkesbury.)

This large church has an unusual chancel:

the parapet and pinnacles are a Victorian oddity which has a certain charm. Inside, the main interest lies in the outstanding collection of Dowdeswell family monuments, the most decorative being a relief of a seated grieving widow leaning against a draped urn. The most remarkable single possession, however, is the 1500 brass of a successful wool merchant, Thomas Payne, and his wife Ursula.

Church Lench: All Saints. (West of A435, north of Evesham.)

Church Lench is a hilltop village and the churchyard occupies the summit. There are extensive views north-west to the Abberley Hills and the BBC masts beyond Droitwich. In the shade of old yews are a preaching cross and, near the road, a sundial made from the medieval font replaced in the nineteenth century. Notice also the village school opposite the lychgate with its rows of improving texts along the walls.

Inside, a riot of welcoming colour is provided by the collection of finely embroidered hassocks lining the old panelled pews. The tympanum above the chancel arch has a large wall-painting, rather indistinct although it is only of the nineteenth century. There is a further painting on the south pillar. The font and lid are also nineteenth-century. The large chancel has a high beamed ceiling with stencil work between the beams. The reredos has three scenes carved in oak representing the Feeding of the Five Thousand.

Cleeve Prior: St Andrew. (On B4085, north-east of Evesham.)

The churchyard pathway is lined with massive ancient tombstones, leading to a doorway with a grille in its upper half. Inside, the west end of the Norman nave has a great soaring arch into the bell-tower. There is an ancient font and an attractive single-light window of 1902. The chancel has more good windows, especially the tall three-light east window of 1869.

Clent: St Leonard. (Off A491, south of Stourbridge.)

The big west tower faces a crossroads. The setting is delightful: a sloping site backed by

The hilltop church of All Saints at Church Lench.

trees rising up the slopes of the Clent Hills. The well-kept churchyard runs upwards to give an elevated view of the church and its setting.

Inside, the chancel is several steps up from the nave because of the sloping ground. There are numerous wall tablets and an arch in the north wall to the vestry which contains a single-light memorial window. The north aisle is as tall as the nave and contains a richly coloured three-light window of 1868. Under the tower, the west window has three scenes from the life of Jesus and there is an oval wall tablet with drapery and three cherubs. In the much more modest south aisle the beautiful window commemorating the end of the First World War shows two scenes of a family gathering the grape harvest.

Cotheridge: St Leonard. (Just off A44, west of Worcester.)

The church is set among farmland and orchards. The south tower is most impressive from outside with its huge ancient timbers and wooden door. The superb Norman inte-

rior is entered through the vestry on the north side. Of particular interest are the fifteenth-century floor tiles in the chancel, the seventeenth-century pulpit and the wealth of box pews.

The churchyard is delightful: informally maintained, shaded by great trees and with footpaths setting off across the surrounding countryside.

Croome d'Abitot: St Mary Magdalene (RCF). (East of A38 at OS 150: SO 886450, south-east of Worcester.)

The church was built in 1763 as part of the remodelling of the estate of the sixth Earl of Coventry. The design is Gothick fantasy with elegant windows and plasterwork, the original font from the earlier church and its communion rails and pulpit. The extraordinary feature is the collection of Coventry monuments in the chancel, mostly of the seventeenth century. Possibly the most outstanding is that to the first Lord Coventry, who died in 1639. He reclines, draped in robes, beneath a huge semicircular canopy. Before him are a

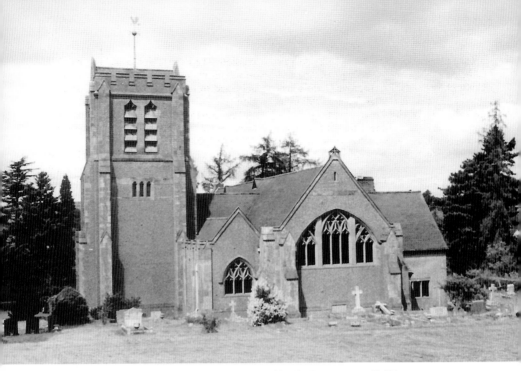

Dodford has an Arts and Crafts church, designed by the Bromsgrove Guild.

cushion and mace. The monument to the sixth Earl (1809) is also striking, showing a kneeling widow bent over a pedestal. The whole collection gives the air of a mausoleum rather than a country church.

Crowle: St John the Baptist. (North of A422, east of Worcester.)

This is a large church with a tall medieval tower. Most of the chancel and nave are late Victorian, but the north porch is fourteenth-century and has figures carved above the entrance. Inside, the lofty nave has good beams and is separated from the chancel by an intricately carved screen, probably of the late nineteenth century. The east window showing the Crucifixion is notable, but it is the marble lectern which provides the main point of interest, with its oddly kneeling figure facing the congregation. It was found lying in the churchyard by a vicar in 1845.

The church is situated just off the village street, which has some good timber-framed houses interspersed with more recent buildings. A number of footpaths lead off the street.

Dodderhill: St Augustine. (Near Droitwich.)

The huge tower dominates the view on a hillside overlooking Droitwich but this is an odd church: the nave has gone and we are left with a north transept, chancel, and the tower where the south transept should be. The walls are massive but the ground underneath is too soft and the whole tower is kept together with steel tie-rods. The nave, south transept and tower were all destroyed or demolished as the result of a Civil War engagement.

The interior, although light and spacious, has a rather forlorn air: there is patching up in the north transept and chancel and the only monument of note has its principal effigy missing. There are fragments of old glass in one window. The absence of the nave gives a somewhat unsatisfactory feel to the place.

The view from the south side of the churchyard is enjoyable, looking over central Droitwich. In the foreground is the restored Droitwich Canal with its basin along to the right.

Dodford: Holy Trinity and St Mary. (North of A448, north-west of Bromsgrove.)

On a pleasant conifer-planted hillside, this is the county's main example of an Arts and Crafts church – the Bromsgrove Guild's version of neo-Gothic (1908). Visitors will form their own impressions regarding the exterior appearance and its fitness for its surroundings. The cloister joining the south tower to the main entrance at the south-west corner of the nave encloses a small courtyard with an open-air pulpit at the base of the tower.

Inside, the church will not disappoint those who enjoy this period. The nave looks east to the chancel under a striking, richly decorated rood beam. The arches of the nave roof are decorated with square Gothic bosses and the windows are enjoyable. The font is in an apse at the west end. A screen next to the entrance door is a fine recent piece, constructed to match the pulpit. There is an organ loft at first-floor level in a north transept, opposite the transept leading to the tower base which culminates in a grand rose window facing south. The chancel has a barrel roof and the whole interior has a wealth of decoration repaying detailed study.

Dormston: St Nicholas. (North of A422, west of Inkberrow.)

This delightful little church is more enjoyable outside than in. The highlight is the charming timber-framed west tower, leaning somewhat on its stone base. Also notable outside are the yews framing the entrance, instead of a lychgate; the heavily timbered south porch, possibly as early as 1350; and the sundial on the wall to the right of the porch.

Inside, the two main points of interest are the heavy timber bracings of the tower and the half dozen ancient pews, roughly hewn, one of which contains a scratched circular maze and animal figures.

Evesham: All Saints.

This is the parish church of Evesham. Of the original, late twelfth-century building consisting of nave and chancel, only the west wall and entrance arch remain. The visitor enters through an outer porch built by Abbot Lichfield between 1500 and 1510. It contains a particularly fine ceiling boss of Christ's passion. The inner porch contains a number of interesting examples of carved stonework salvaged from the abbey church at demolition.

The present nave, south aisle and south transept are fifteenth-century. The Lichfield Chapel off the south aisle is particularly beautiful, with a memorable fan-vaulted ceiling. It dates from around 1510 and was built by Abbot Lichfield for his own burial: his remains are beneath the floor.

Most of the remainder of the building is Victorian, dating from Preedy's restoration of 1873-6: the chancel, north aisle and north transept all belong to this period. The stone pulpit is to his design (1875), with the four gospellers carved in marble. The rood screen (1905) was carved locally and the crucifix suspended above the screen came from Oberammergau.

The stained glass windows will remain in many visitors' minds. Apart from a single medieval one, they are all Victorian and extend around the whole building, depicting scenes from both Old and New Testaments as well as events in the history and legend of Evesham. A guide to the windows is available in the church.

Evesham: St Lawrence.

Declared redundant in 1978, the church underwent major restoration work in 1994-5. It has had a chequered history since it was first mentioned in 1195. Before the Dissolution in 1540, St Lawrence enjoyed considerable prestige. After the abbey's demise, endowments decreased, the building deteriorated and by 1718 it was virtually unusable in winter. A public appeal launched in 1730-1 produced sufficient funds to enable restoration to begin in 1737. Disaster struck when the new roof collapsed within a few years and the building was abandoned. With few free seats at All Saints, the town's poorer inhabitants deserted the Church of England: by the 1780s more than a quarter of Evesham's population were dissenters.

Edmund Rudge, squire of Evesham, promoted a thorough restoration, undertaken in 1836-7 by Eginton. The building today reflects that restoration: the tower and south of aisle are fifteenth-century; the south chapel is sixteenth-century and the nave, chancel and north aisle are all Eginton's work. Being traditionally low-church and, in the eyes of many, inferior to neighbouring All Saints, St Lawrence received far fewer gifts of Victorian glass and furnishings. The result today is a building full of light with clean soaring lines. The aisles, extending almost the whole length of the nave and chancel, give a feeling of almost cathedral dimensions.

Great Comberton: St Michael. (South of A44, south of Pershore.)

The church is up a lane just off the main street. The lane and especially the main street have a good variety of well-kept houses. The path leads through yew trees to a doorway unusually in the west wall of the tower. Inside, the impression is also unusual: the tower space, nave and chancel are almost all in one,

with little apparent division. The nave has impressive curved timber beams and a wealth of plain sixteenth-century pews. In the chancel the stalls have carved Jacobean panels. The most enjoyable feature is the windows: they all contain nineteenth-century designs.

Great Malvern: Priory Church of St Mary and St Michael.

The greater part of this priory church was saved from destruction by the parishioners of Great Malvern in 1541. The Lady Chapel and south transept had already been demolished when Henry VIII's commissioners accepted an offer of £20 for what remained, payable in two instalments.

Externally the church is Perpendicular (about 1420-60). The tall tower, surmounted by pierced battlements and pinnacles, dominates the centre of Great Malvern. Inside, the visitor is immediately impressed by the sense

The Priory Church of St Mary and St Michael at Great Malvern.

The monument to the first Lord Foley at Great Witley church is the tallest funerary monument in England.

strength and space. The strength comes from the massive low Norman pillars; the space from the soaring clerestory windows high above the pillars. The ceilings are flat in the nave and chancel, with squared timbering; the aisles have floral painting and gilded bosses and there is fan vaulting under the crossing tower.

The windows contain the most complete collection of fifteenth-century stained glass in all England. Largest of all is the great west window (about 1460-80), followed by the east window (about 1440) and a whole series of windows around the chancel and north transept.

Another unique feature of the church is the collection of some twelve hundred wall tiles on the chancel screens. These are also fifteenth-century and the only church wall tiles in England. Other features of interest include the misericords in the choir stalls, the mosaic reredos (1884) and a number of chest tombs and wall monuments. The white marble memorial to Sophia Thompson (died 1836), showing a female figure reclining on a couch, is especially fine.

The only surviving monastic building is the Gatehouse, which now accommodates the Malvern Museum (page 86). Its north side, facing the town, is of elaborately carved stone but it has a plainer façade, partly of brick, on the outer side. The roadway runs through an arch beneath the upper storey.

Great Witley: St Michael. (At junction of A451 and A443, south-west of Stourport.)

The church is immediately adjacent to ruined Witley Court (page 79) and is one of the sights not to be missed in Worcestershire. Thomas, first Lord Foley, caused the church to be built and it was consecrated in 1736, three years after his death. Its external appearance is plain, even forbidding, especially in the context of the neighbouring ruins.

Nothing outside prepares the first-time visitor for the revelation on entering: the initial impact is breathtaking. It is invariably described as England's finest baroque church, the creation of the second Lord Foley. The ceiling commands instant attention, with its three large and twenty smaller paintings by the Italian master Antonio Bellucci (born 1654). These and much else besides came from the palace of Canons, near Edgware, Middlesex, which was demolished in 1747. The stucco work surrounding the paintings is actually papier-mâché, an invention of a Birmingham man, Henry Clay, in the mid eighteenth century.

The second outstanding feature is Rysbrack's massive monument to the first Lord Foley, with his reclining figure on a grey sarcophagus and the attendant seated figure of his grieving widow with a child. Other figures, drapery and an urn complete this huge creation, all mounted on a block some 6 feet (2 metres) high. It is the tallest funerary monument in England.

The Victorian paintings, the painted glass,

the pulpit, Handel's organ case – the church is full of treasures, in an unforgettable setting.

Hagley: St John the Baptist. (Near junction of A456 and A491, south of Stourbridge.)

The church occupies a wonderful site, surrounded by Hagley deer park with its obelisks and close to Hagley Hall (page 74). The churchyard is entered by a lychgate covered with improving texts. The tall tower is red sandstone and the building looks like a straightforward Victorian estate church. There is, however, some medieval work remaining, mostly in the south aisle.

The interior is chiefly notable for the stained glass and memorials, mostly to the Lytteltons of Hagley Hall. The chancel east window (1857) shows the Resurrection; the south window (1876) is a memorial to the fourth Baron Lyttelton. There is a cast-iron ornamental screen separating chancel from nave and on the south chancel-arch pillar is a wall memorial to Sybella Lyttelton (1900). Both aisles have stained glass and there is a large west window under the tower. Here also are a whole series of wall tablets and a rather odd decorated urn and putto in marble (1747). To the west of the entrance door a plaque records a visit by Queen Adelaide in 1843.

Harvington (near Evesham): St James. (On B439, north of Evesham.)

Both nave and chancel are very lofty; the latter has curved beams and a large organ casing. There is a tall, highly coloured east window of Christ in Majesty. The two nave windows of 1881 and 1917 are more pleasingly subdued. On the nave south wall is a First World War roll of honour made especially poignant by the accompanying frame which has a photograph of each of the fallen men, all so proud and many very young. The west wall of the nave has two wall monuments of 1619 and 1786.

Himbleton: St Mary Magdalene. (North of A422, north-east of Worcester.)

A timber lychgate leads to a pleasant churchyard and an enjoyable little church. The bell turret has a memorial clock of 1910 and a rather flamboyant scroll on the wall. The heavily timbered fourteenth-century porch protects a low Norman doorway. Inside, nave and chancel are separated only by a high rood beam; sturdy pillars divide nave and north aisle. The windows are mainly nineteenth-century with an impressive Adoration of the Magi in the north aisle and a good east window incorporating some fifteenth-century glass.

Holt: St Martin. (East of A443, north of Worcester.)

This is a fine Norman church which repays attention externally for its intricately carved doorways and window arches. Inside, the great chancel arch has similar contrasting carved courses with a huge mosaic recording the restoration in 1859. The carved stone is of

The bell turret at Himbleton.

similar date.

The chancel east window (1897) commemorates Charles Sale, rector here for forty-nine years. Two more nineteenth-century mosaics flank the window. In the north wall is a richly carved Norman doorway. The south chapel has old floor tiles and inscribed tomb lids: on the west wall is an interesting memorial of 1704 with spiral columns and cherub heads. Below is a memorable effigy of a lady thought to be a member of the Beauchamp family in the fifteenth century, her devout air reaching us across the centuries. Under the great west tower is the striking Norman font with barbaric masks of feline faces tied together with tendrils curving round the bowl.

Opposite the weathered sandstone lychgate, and behind two huge cedars, is Holt Castle (page 52).

Huddington: St James. (North of A422, east of Worcester.)

The church is memorably situated, close to the picturesque Huddington Court. Cars should be left on the public road. The churchyard has a carved lychgate, crucifix, large eighteenth-century chest tombs and yew trees. The church is small and simple, with a timber-framed bell turret and fourteenth-century wooden porch.

Inside, the nave has impressive curved beams. The three-light east window depicts the Crucifixion and there are brasses set in the panelled chancel walls, the largest of 1653. The stalls, communion rail, rood screen and pulpit are all pleasant, ancient and fairly plain. The south aisle has similarly simple old box pews, two chests, one ancient with twin lids, the other of 1909 and finely carved, and a canvas of the Last Supper hangs on the south wall.

Inkberrow: St Peter. (On A422, east of Worcester.)

The stone porch has battlements, pinnacles and interesting, rather weathered gargoyles. Inside is a carved wooden screen of 1970 and an unusually square, early thirteenth-century font. The chancel has two good windows portraying saints but the south transept houses the greatest treasure: the ornate alabaster tomb effigy of John Savage, High Sheriff of Worcestershire, who died in 1631. The effigy detail is particularly fine and the whole monument incorporates many enjoyable features.

The church, inn and buildings round the village green make this a pleasant spot to linger, far enough set back from the busy Worcester to Stratford-upon-Avon road.

Kidderminster: St Mary.

Prominently sited on a hill above the town centre, Worcestershire's largest parish church has much to interest visitors. Externally the church is dominated by its heavily buttressed four-stage tower. Both tower and nave are battlemented and, east of the nave, the church is unusual in having chancel, sanctuary, cloistered vestry and chantry, which more than double the building's length.

Inside, the nave is surrounded by nineteenth-century stained glass, in the three west windows and in the closely set clerestory windows leading up to the flat timber ceiling. The 1873 font is surrounded by a striking metal sculpture installed in 1992. The stone pulpit is decorated with carved saints. The octagonal pillars are concave on each face.

The chancel contains three magnificent tomb monuments: two for the Blount family (sixteenth- and seventeenth-century) and one for Sir Hugh Cokesey (died 1445) and his wife Alice. Against the south wall is the tomb of Lady Joyce Beauchamp (died 1473); a superb example of fifteenth-century monumental art. By the communion rail is the Cokesey brass of Lady Matilda Phelip flanked by her two husbands. Of the early fourteenth century, it is as fine a brass as any in Worcestershire.

The Whittall Chapel should not be missed: it is entered through a curtained doorway in the chancel north wall. Designed by Sir Charles Gilbert Scott and completed in 1922, the chapel was paid for by Matthew Whittall, a Kidderminster man who emigrated to Massachusetts and made a fortune in carpet manufacturing. Of particular interest is the reredos showing Christ preaching in Galilee. It is intricately carved in oak with gold gilding. Also notable are the three windows installed by Whittall's widow in his memory: they depict the Virgin Mary, Joan of Arc and Florence Nightingale and are quite beautiful.

Another fine reredos is located behind the high altar in the chancel. It shows the Last Supper and is an outstanding example of high Victorian sculpture. The main scene is surmounted by a richly ornamented ogee arch and backed by a tall six-light east window.

Beyond the high altar is the mid sixteenth-century chantry, which has excellent painted ceiling beams. Now serving as a parish hall, it was the town's grammar school for over two hundred years until new premises were built in 1843.

Leigh: St Eadburga. (West of A4103, west of Worcester.)

This is one of the county's finest village churches, with good Norman work both outside and in. The chancel has three magnificent monuments: here are William and Mary Colles kneeling in life-size effigy, with their twelve children lined along the tomb chest; opposite lie Sir Walter and Lady Devereux, carved in alabaster.

The Lady Chapel has more delights: a twelfth-century stone figure of Christ, mounted above the altar; and the wonderful fifteenth-century rood screen decorated with Tudor roses. Of particular note are the grand columns with large square capitals.

Adjacent to the churchyard are Leigh Court, a long brick mansion with stepped gables, two lodge houses and the great cruck barn (page 52).

Little Comberton: St Peter. (South of A44, south-east of Pershore.)

The tall tower has impressive gargoyles. Entry is through a porch of 1639, with an unusual tympanum over the doorway. The interior gives the impression of being heavily restored. The chancel was rebuilt in 1886 and there are enjoyable windows in the east and north walls and good carving above the altar.

The churchyard is shaded by huge firs. There is an enjoyable short circular walk around Manor Lane which has an excellent variety of timber-framed and thatched cottages.

Little Malvern: Priory Church of St Giles. (At junction of A449 and A4104, south of Great Malvern.)

The setting for this church is delightful, particularly when approached from the east along the A4104 from Upton upon Severn. The church and neighbouring Little Malvern Court (page 78) form a picturesque group against the background of the Malvern Hills. Close to, and inside, the church presents a rather forlorn appearance: only the chancel, crossing tower and small south transept remain, the rest having been demolished after the Dissolution in the 1530s. This was the church of a Benedictine priory which had been founded by 1171, perhaps some fifty years earlier.

A small monastery, never accommodating more than a dozen monks at a time, Little Malvern was subject to the see of Worcester. In 1480 Bishop Alcock found the monastery poorly maintained and administered and he dispatched the monks to Gloucester for two years as a punishment, while restoration work was undertaken.

The nave and north transept were demolished at the Dissolution along with all the domestic buildings except for the refectory or prior's hall. This is now incorporated in Little Malvern Court.

Inside the church the chancel has been divided by a rood screen and part of an intricately carved rood beam. There are some ancient stalls, partly mutilated by having the misericords chopped off, and some old glass remains in two windows.

Martley: St Peter. (On B4204, north-west of Worcester.)

This is an impressively large village church with a soaring red sandstone tower which glows in the sunlight. The nave and chancel are Norman and very spacious inside, with impressive beams in the lofty ceilings. There is excellent carving in the seventeenth-century tympanum which separates nave from chancel and good painted stencil work in the chancel, particularly on the north wall. On the south side of the chancel is a finely detailed alabaster figure of a knight in armour, commemorating Hugh Mortimer, who fell at the

Pershore Abbey from the south-east.

battle of Wakefield in 1459, supporting the Yorkist cause.

Outside there are extensive views across the surrounding farmland, and the church makes a pleasant group with the nearby rectory and village school just up the hill.

Middle Littleton: St Nicholas. (On B4085, north-east of Evesham.)

The historic part of the village, around the church, is all Cotswold stone, including the great tithe barn (page 53). The church contains a number of interesting features, including: the old box pews, originally fifteenth-century; the pulpit, half an octagon and made from fifteenth-century panels; the altar reredos; the carved surround of the west doorway; and especially the Norman font. In the churchyard the shaft and base of the original preaching cross are near a huge yew.

Oddingley: St James. (South of B4090, south of Droitwich.)

An enjoyable little church, extensively restored in the nineteenth century, St James is tucked behind the fine brick barns of Church Farm. It occupies a hilltop site looking down on the Worcester & Birmingham Canal and with extensive views westward to the

Malverns. The painted glass, mostly fifteenth-century, is a great treasure for such a modest edifice, particularly the east window. Most has been collected from other windows. There are a number of fitments from nearby Hadzor church, closed in 1970, and, behind the seventeenth-century communion rail, a memorial to a rector, George Parker, murdered in 1806 apparently as the result of a tithe dispute.

Pershore: Abbey Church of the Holy Cross with St Eadburga.

The abbey is thought to have been founded in the late seventh century and had a turbulent history until about 1100, when the Norman community was established. At the Dissolution in 1539 the nave and Lady Chapel, together with all the monastic buildings, were demolished. An initial walk around the outside enables the visitor to see what remains and gain some impression of what was lost.

At the east end, nearest the street, is a semicircular apse (1846) built on the site of the demolished Lady Chapel. Proceeding round to the right, the various features of the north side include flying buttresses supporting the battlemented chancel and a vestry (1936) built on the site of the north transept, which collapsed in the 1680s. The former roofline can still be seen on the tower wall. Beside the vestry is a massive buttress, built in 1686 to support the tower after the transept collapsed.

On the south side, a pair of ornamental gates marks the position of the former west door of the nave, which doubles the length of the present building to some 325 feet (100 metres): Worcester Cathedral is 387 feet (118 metres). Here two more large buttresses (1913) support the west side of the tower, on which the nave roofline and curved outline of the arch leading from the tower to the nave can be seen.

To the right is the south transept, the oldest part of the building (eleventh- to twelfth-century). Low down on the west of the wall of the transept is the roofline of the cloisters and higher up on the south wall is the roofline of the monks' dormitory. It was here, to the south and west of the church, that all the now vanished buildings of the monastery were located.

The visitor entering the abbey church by the western door is immediately aware of the superb vaulting of the chancel roof, the joints embellished with intricately carved bosses, but far too high for the individual details to be discerned by the naked eye. This is thirteenth-century building at its best, the slender columns leading up to the tall windows and wonderful roof.

Almost equally impressive is the spectacle up the west tower, completed about 1330. It is open to its second stage, where a nineteenth-century suspended ringing platform was installed. The tower has high soaring arches, one leading to the Norman south transept, which houses a number of points of interest: a

monument to a Knight Templar (about 1280); an ornate Elizabethan monument to Thomas Haselwood, whose recumbent form is accompanied by two kneeling figures, all wonderfully detailed; a modern war memorial and a showcase containing the charter granted to the Benedictine monks by King Edgar in 927.

The font is Norman and was thrown out in 1840 when a new one was installed. It was found in a garden in Kempsey village in 1920 and reinstated in its rightful place. In St Michael's Chapel there is a floor of medieval tiles and a window by Kempe (about 1885). Further windows of 1870 in the chancel show the story of St Eadburga and events in the history of Pershore.

Pirton: St Peter. (East of A38, south-east of Worcester.)

An entirely unexpected feature of this well-kept little church is the superb fourteenth-century timber-framed tower with large cruck-type beams forming two aisles at its lower level. The tower is set against the north wall of the Norman nave. Above the south door is a Norman gargoyle, the sole survivor of an original seven representing the deadly sins.

Inside are an oak chest and finely carved chair, both of around 1675. The octagonal pulpit is good Jacobean work and the east window is a colourful late nineteenth-century design. The well-maintained churchyard is surrounded by pleasant rolling farmland.

Rock: St Peter. (South of A456, south-west of Bewdley.)

This imposing Norman church of about 1170 occupies a most prominent hill site which emphasises its lofty proportions. The entrance is by a most elaborate north doorway with quadruple courses of fine carving surmounted by a triangular pediment. To the left, each of the two clerestory windows has its east light blocked up, an odd feature.

Inside, the lofty nave is separated from the chancel by a tall arch with splendid intricate carving on the capitals. The tall pillars of the south aisle are octagonal with concave capitals. The font in the south aisle is twelfth-century on a nineteenth-century base. The east window of the chancel (1894) is a striking three-light representation of Christ preaching. There are two further, highly coloured windows in the chancel north wall. The south chapel, separated from the chancel by a glass screen, contains a number of points of interest: an ancient altar slab on a modern base, the stone Coningsby tomb and a collection of wall memorials.

The churchyard has a number of substantial tombs and gives extensive views. From the south-east corner there is a clear view of a moated platform, the site of a once substantial fortified enclosure.

Salwarpe: St Michael. (West of A38, south-west of Droitwich.)

The Droitwich Canal runs in a deep cutting beside the churchyard, which is approached through a timbered lychgate and an archway of yews. There is a preaching cross and a number of interesting old tombs and large yews crowd against the base of the tall battlemented tower. The south porch entrance leads into a buttressed south aisle.

The east window showing the Crucifixion is impressive and there are three more mid nineteenth-century windows. The altar reredos has an alabaster group of the Last Supper and, on the chancel south wall, Thomas Talbot and his wife (1613) kneel facing each other, with their three children kneeling below them. The eastern ends of both aisles have chapels, or family pews. That of 1681 in the south aisle has an inscribed tomb chest of black and white marble to Olave Talbot and her mother Elizabeth. Timber-framed Salwarpe Court, the Talbot family

home, can be seen from the road across the canal bridge.

Shelsley Beauchamp: All Saints. (North of B4204, north-west of Worcester.)

Here is an impressive red sandstone tower, probably fourteenth-century, but the remainder of the building is early Victorian (1846-7) and lacks the intimate charm of the neighbouring church of Shelsley Walsh, which lies just across the Teme and is reached by New Mill Bridge a short distance downstream. The setting of the churchyard and neighbouring Georgian rectory are extremely pleasant, however, and there is a good view over the delightful Teme valley.

Shelsley Walsh: St Andrew. (North of B4204, north-west of Worcester.)

This is a gem of a church, delightfully situated in the Teme valley. The simple tufa exterior conceals a wealth of treasures. Chancel and nave are separated by a fifteenth-century oak screen surmounted by the original, intricately carved rood beam and a nineteenth-century Celtic-style cross. The screen continues to enclose a small chantry chapel. Sir Francis Walsh has an excellent wooden tomb of 1596: coats of arms adorn the sides. The nave roof timbers are particularly impressive and an unusual feature is the wooden

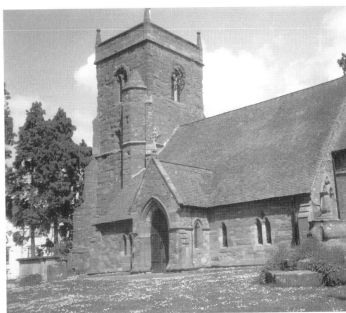

In the Teme valley is the sandstone church at Shelsley Beauchamp.

The inscription over the south doorway at St Mary's church, Shrawley.

beam which slides across the medieval oak door to give added protection when churches were a place of sanctuary.

Shrawley: St Mary. (West of B4196, south of Stourport.)

This is a large Norman church set in a pleasant churchyard with seats on the rising ground behind the church. Remains of an external frieze can be seen at intervals around the building. At the entrance is a Gothick-looking house set in a beautiful cottage garden. To the right is the well-worn base of a preaching cross.

Spetchley: All Saints (RCF). (On A422, east of Worcester.)

The church adjoins Spetchley Park (page 78). It is a simple early fourteenth-century building with a superb chapel added in 1614. It houses a remarkable collection of monuments to the Berkeley family, owners of Spetehley Park. There are good effigies and particularly fine heraldry. The alabaster monument to Sir Rowland Berkeley, died 1611, is notable: he lies with his wife under an arched canopy with obelisks at each corner.

Stockton on Teme: St Andrew. (On A443, east of Tenbury Wells.)

This delightful little Norman church stands on a steeply sloping site. The brick-built chancel is early eighteenth-century and there is a timber campanile. Of particular interest are the splendidly sculpted Norman south doorway and chancel arch and, particularly, the superb wooden tomb chest of Thomas Walsh (died 1593) with its finely detailed coats of arms. There is a similar monument at Shelsley Walsh a little further down the Teme valley.

The neighbouring farm has some impressive ranges of brick-built farm buildings, and the tree-shaded churchyard is a pleasant place to linger.

Stoke Prior: St Nicholas. (On B4091, south of Bromsgrove.)

This imposing church stands in a large well-kept churchyard on a hilltop site above the little river Salwarpe. The carved timber lychgate frames a Celtic cross monument raised after the First World War. The splendid tower is placed to the south side of the church, where a transept should be: it has a hipped, shingled spire. The south aisle is battlemented and short, only two bays, joining the tower and south porch.

The interior is dominated by the unfortunately large and highly coloured east window of 1860. It was a tribute to John Corbett (page 103) in recognition of his decision not to permit women and children to work any longer in his salt pits, 1 mile (2 km) south of here (page 97). In the south aisle is a much defaced stone effigy of a thirteenth-century priest.

Stone: St Mary. (On A448, east of Kidderminster.)

The entrance is through the tall, pinnacled west tower. The interior is spacious and light and the east window is enjoyable. The main interest lies in the churchyard and pleasant surroundings. There are a number of interesting tombs and monuments: the large Gibbons tomb (nineteenth-century); the 1788 memorial plinth to little Hannah Hill, who died aged seven; the preaching cross and a number of other interesting memorials grouped round a twisted yew. The partly timbered former village school and a good range of brick barns border the churchyard.

Tardebigge: St Bartholemew. (On A448, east of Bromsgrove.)

This is a large and extremely interesting church occupying a magnificent site. The extensive churchyard contains a number of enjoyable features, including a secluded memorial and graves for the family of the Earls of Plymouth, a well-worn preaching cross and a series of panoramic views across the Severn lowlands. This is the edge of the Midlands plateau. The local primary school lies along one side of the churchyard, much extended from its earlier 1845 building.

From the outside, the great tower, crowned by a needle spire, commands attention. Built in 1777, the bell stage has concave sides and columns, surrounded by urns. The interior is light and somewhat plain but towards the eastern end of the church, added in 1879-80, is a feast of good things. To the south of the chancel arch is an impressive wall memorial to the dead of two world wars, the rolls of honour surmounted by carved draped flags. North of the arch is a family pew. Above it, in the north wall, is a most impressive window

of 1894 to Jane and Susanna, the two wives of Thomas Dixon, who presumably outlived them both. To the right is the late seventeenth-century memorial to Lady Mary Cookes and her husband; they are holding hands and he sports an impressive curled wig. The monument is extremely ornate, with twisted columns, attendant figures, a coat of arms and a most interesting inscription. Beneath is the family pew and, in the floor, a brass records that below is the vault of the Cookes family, reputed to have come to England with the Conqueror.

The chancel stalls and prayer desk are finely carved and are a tribute to a vicar who, in 1907, had ministered in this church for fifty years. The chancel ends in an apse and the east window shows the Pentecost scene. It is on the south side of the chancel, however, that the great treasure of Tardebigge church is found. The sixth Earl of Plymouth died prematurely at the age of forty-four, in 1833. The white marble monument, by Chantry, portrays his distraught grieving widow. That superb craftsman has created a deeply moving sculpture that conveys the sense of loss his young widow felt all those years ago.

From the churchyard a footpath leads down to the Worcester & Birmingham Canal near the top of the great flight of locks up from the Severn lowlands (page 97).

Warndon: St Nicholas. (North-east of Worcester.)

The early twelfth-century nave forms a continuous unit with the chancel, rebuilt in the fifteenth century. The lower part of the nave wall is built of lias stone, the upper part of red Bromsgrove stone, rendered with plaster. Inside there are seventeenth-century box pews and a barrel ceiling of lath and plaster. The restored east window of the nave contains fourteenth-century glass. The fifteenth-century font is of a rare seven-sided design. The tower, at the west end, was built in the sixteenth century and is timber-framed with lath and plaster infill. The timber porch was added in the seventeenth century, infilled with brick the following century. Outside, on a buttress on the south wall of the nave, is a scratch dial, a primitive form of sundial used to indicate the time of Mass.

Wilden: All Saints. (West of A449, north-east of Stourport.)

With the revival of interest in the Pre-Raphaelite movement, many visitors to Worcestershire will wish to visit this church. Outwardly unremarkable, it has an interior that is unique in Worcestershire and probably without parallel anywhere. The whole place is a memorial to the Baldwin family (page 103), and the remarkable Macdonald sisters to whom they were related. The stained glass windows are a gallery of the work of William Morris and Sir Edward Burne-Jones, although both men were dead when the windows were actually made in 1900-14.

The church was built in 1880 for the local ironmaster Alfred Baldwin, father of Stanley. His wife, Louisa, was the sister of Georgiana Burne-Jones, whose husband was commissioned to design all the windows. The chancel and nave are all in one, separated by a rail. At the east end is a three-light window: Jesus with children flanked by St Martin and St George. Below, the wall either side of the altar is hung with tapestry designed by William Morris. On the north wall is a glass case holding a heavy tapestry, also designed by Morris, worked in gold thread by Louisa Baldwin, Georgiana Burne-Jones and Edith Macdonald. To the right is a marble wall memorial to Alfred Baldwin, who died in 1908. His ironworks were just along the road towards Kidderminster.

The front south pew was where the Baldwin family sat: here are three brasses to them, including Prime Minister Stanley Baldwin, first Earl Baldwin of Bewdley, who died in 1947. There are numerous other brasses around the nave walls, including one to Alice and John Lockwood Kipling, parents of Rudyard; Alice was another of the Macdonald sisters. Yet another sister, Agnes, is commemorated on one of the windows: she was the wife of Sir Edward Poynter, President of the Royal Academy, and died in 1906.

Of the other windows two are particularly notable: the large west window commemorating three friends of Alfred Baldwin, and the memorial window to Alfred himself and his wife Louisa. Her panels are particularly attractive and unusual, being composed of foliage and floral motifs.

This church should not be missed by those who have an interest in the art of the period and for the interrelated families it commemorates.

Worcester Cathedral: the Blessed Virgin Mary.

The Worcester Cathedral we see today is largely a product of the great Victorian restoration which commenced in 1854 and continued for some twenty years. This has given the cathedral a look and feel that, with the revival of interest in the Victorian period, the great majority of visitors will enjoy.

The best point of entry is the splendid north porch, which brings the visitor into the western end of the nave. Here it is suggested that you walk to the centre and look both east and west, and up, to gain a first impression of the wonderful size and proportions of the main body of the building. The cathedral has an overall length of 387 feet (118 metres) and the nave is 68 feet (21 metres) high. The west window, one of the most glorious in any cathedral, has eight vertical lights surmounted by a huge rose, depicting the Creation. To the right is a fine seated monument to Bishop Henry Philpott and nearby is the lovely 'Dream of Gerontius' memorial window and plaque to Sir Edward Elgar (page 103).

If a clockwise route is now followed, starting by walking east along the north aisle, there is the Beauchamp monument with Sir John and his wife side by side. A favourite of Richard II, Sir John fell foul of the Merciless Parliament in 1388 and was executed. In the north quire aisle is a superb model of the cathedral made by a local man, Mr A. T. Harley. Completed in 1984, it took 15,300 hours of painstaking work.

St George's Chapel in the north-east corner of the quire is a memorial to local service men and women. There are numerous colours hanging and some excellent windows. Opposite the chapel is a fine memorial to Lord Littleton, brother-in-law to Gladstone and a substantial contributor to the Victorian restoration. This memorial is by Sir Gilbert Scott and there is another, on the far side of the quire, to the first Earl of Dudley, who lived at Witley Court.

The cloisters and herb garden at Worcester Cathedral.

The Lady Chapel gives the opportunity to view the great east window, the reverse side of the marble reredos behind the high altar and, with the aid of a tilted mirror, the wonderful painted ceiling of the quire.

In the south quire aisle is Prince Arthur's Chantry. Here lies the elder son of Henry VII, whose premature death gave his younger brother, Henry VIII, the throne of England and his new bride Catherine of Aragon. Thus the history of English religion was changed.

Beneath the quire is the largest Norman crypt in England; it is the oldest part of the cathedral (begun in 1084). Above, before the high altar, is the tomb of King John, buried here, in accordance with his wishes, in 1216.

The nave pulpit deserves close inspection for its extraordinarily rich carving in alabaster, supported on marble legs. It was donated by the first Earl of Dudley.

From the south aisle a door leads into the cloisters. Immediately on the right is the gift shop and on the eastern side is the chapterhouse, the earliest in Britain to be built round, with a single central pillar. As you walk along the cloisters, look up at the wealth of intricately carved roof bosses.

An arched passageway in the south-east corner of the cloisters leads out to College Green. Immediately to the right is the large College Hall, formerly the monks' refectory, and now the school hall for King's School. The majority of the school buildings are on the far side of College Green.

An interesting area lies to the right of College Green. Here a path leads down under a low arch to the ferry steps on the bank of the Severn. A wide promenade leads both up and down stream. At the west end of the cathedral are some pleasant gardens overlooking the Severn and the ruins of the Guesten Hall, formerly a lodging house for visitors to the monastery. The magnificent timber roof of the hall is now preserved and displayed at Avoncroft Museum of Historic Buildings, Bromsgrove (page 85).

Worcester: St Swithun (RCF).

Rebuilt, except for its Tudor tower, in 1734-6, this is an almost unaltered early Georgian church. It has all the appropriate furnishings, including box pews and a magnificent three-decker pulpit under a rich tester, surmounted by a gilded pelican feeding her young. There is also the Mayor's pew and the whole interior and furnishings are notable for the high quality of their craftsmanship.

6
Historic houses and gardens

Abberley Hall, Abberley, Worcester WR6 6DD (OS 138: SO 747668). Telephone: 01299 896634. On A443 8 miles (13 km) south-west of Stourport-on-Severn.

Open: mid July to end of August, weekdays.

This is an Italianate house built around 1846 and now a school. Visitors are taken on conducted tours of five of the main rooms. The clock-tower (1883) designed by St Aubyn stands near the house and is a landmark for miles around.

Berkeley's Hospital and Chapel, The Foregate, Worcester.

Open: at any reasonable time – apply to Warden.

Founded in 1697 and completed in 1703, Berkeley's Hospital is just off one of the busiest thoroughfares in Worcester's city centre. A pair of ornate tall cast-iron gates with the words 'Berkeleys Hospital' and the family coat of arms give access to a long quadrangle of grass and flower beds. Single-storey almshouses line either side of the quadrangle and at the far end is a tall chapel building with an excellent statue of the founder, Robert Berkeley, in an apse above the door.

The architecture is in the style of the end of the seventeenth century: perfect symmetry with a strong Dutch influence. Robert Berkeley, of Spetchley Park near Worcester, was ambassador to the Stadtholder of Holland (later William III of England) and had developed an admiration for Dutch architecture. Admission to the chapel can be arranged on application to the Warden's house, immediately on the left inside the gate.

It is fortunate that the gates survived the Second World War. They were dismantled and hidden shortly before a gang arrived to cart them off to aid the munitions drive!

Burford House Gardens, Burford, Tenbury Wells WR15 8HQ (OS 138: SO 581679). Telephone: 01584 810777. On A456 2 miles (3 km) west of Tenbury Wells.

Open: daily.

This is a delightful 4 acre (2 hectare) garden beside the river Teme, created over the past forty years by the late John Treasure. It contains rare and specimen trees, shrubs and plants, plus the National Clematis Collection. A further area with formal pools lies outside the garden, together with a large plant centre, restaurant, gallery and craft shop.

Countess of Huntingdon's Hall, Crowngate, Worcester WR1 3LD. Telephone: 01905 611427.

Open: daily on application.

One of the finest examples of nonconformist architecture in Britain, this hall was threatened with demolition, but a spirited and determined campaign by Worcester Civic Society earned it a reprieve. £500,000 was raised to recreate the interior, described by John Betjeman as 'unique and irreplaceable'.

Selina, Countess of Huntingdon (1707-91), devoted her life to combatting the reckless atheism prevalent among the eighteenth-century upper classes. Her influence was countrywide and for a time she worked with John Wesley.

The somewhat plain appearance of the building does nothing to prepare the visitor for its superb interior with a curving gallery supported on slender columns and the magnificent Nicholson organ, now fully restored.

Today the hall, with an additional building housing a restaurant and exhibition, sits most comfortably in a square at the heart of the new Crowngate development. It is home to the thriving Elgar Music School and a venue for an extremely varied programme of musical occasions, including lunchtime performances.

Eastgrove Cottage Garden Nursery, Sankyns Green, Little Witley, Worcester WR6 6LQ (OS 138: SO 793643). Telephone: 01299 896389. On the road between Shrawley (on B4196) and Great Witley (on A443).
Open: April to July, Thursday to Monday afternoons; September to mid October, Thursday to Saturday afternoons. Closed in August.

This is a traditional country flower garden surrounding a seventeenth-century timber-framed yeoman farmhouse. The planting arrangements emphasise colour and form and there is an expanding collection of hardy plants with a wide range of less usual varieties. The garden is set in 5 acres (2 hectares) of meadow and woodland. Plants are sold from the nursery.

The Greyfriars, Friar Street, Worcester. Telephone: 01905 23571. National Trust.
Open: Easter Monday to end of October, Wednesday, Thursday and bank holiday Monday afternoons.

This is one of Worcestershire's finest surviving timber-framed buildings, dating from about 1480. It was possibly the guest-house of the friary which was built here after the Franciscans arrived in Worcester in 1239. The street frontage consists of two Elizabethan wings separated by an archway into the rear courtyard. Inside, the best room,

Berkeley's Hospital and Chapel in the Foregate, Worcester.

Hagley Hall.

reached by an Elizabethan staircase, is above the entrance hall and part of the archway. It contains an attractive plaster frieze and, unusually, a ceiling dating from the time the room was created. Several of the panelled rooms contain interesting textiles and furnishings and a beautiful secluded walled garden has been created behind the house.

Hagley Hall, Hagley DY9 9LG. Telephone: 01562 882408. 7 miles (11 km) north-east of Kidderminster, off A456.
Open: mid July to end of August, afternoons; also bank holiday weekends.

Hagley Hall and Park are largely the creation of George, first Lord Lyttelton (1709-73), who began to landscape the grounds in the picturesque style in 1751 and built the house between 1756 and 1760. The estate had belonged to the Lyttelton family since 1564 and an earlier house, or hunting lodge, stood on what is now the cricket ground, near the present house. Hagley Hall was the last of the great Palladian houses, employing Italian and English craftsmen to create the plasterwork which is an outstanding feature of the house.

Visitors are conducted through a series of rooms. The library and boudoir contain many family portraits. The Barrel Room, created after a disastrous fire in 1925, has a curved Jacobean-style plaster ceiling and rich Tudor panelling salvaged from the old hunting lodge; it accommodates an extension of the library.

The state dining room was designed as an eighteenth-century saloon with windows giving extensive views across the park. The rococo ceiling, created by Vassalli in 1758-9, has winged putti flying among clouds. The walls have festoons of plasterwork with trophies representing the first Lord Lyttelton's wide-ranging interests. These festoons provide the framework for a further series of family portraits.

The Tapestry Dining Room is another remarkable rococo room conceived by Lord Lyttelton. Originally woven in 1725, the six tapestries were acquired by the family in 1752 and the room was designed to accommodate them. The ceiling has four zephyrs in medallions at its corners and a centrepiece of Flora, the flower goddess, painted on canvas.

Along the whole length of the house is the gallery, now restored after having been used for cricket practice by nineteenth-century members of the family. Originally intended for the display of paintings and sculpture, the gallery is 86 feet (26 metres) long and lit by chandeliers of Waterford crystal.

The park contains a large deer herd and numerous park buildings: the Temple of Theseus, a castle, an obelisk and the Prince of Wales's Column. Near the house is the estate church of St John the Baptist (page 62).

Hanbury Hall, Hanbury, Droitwich WR9 7EA. Telephone: 01527 821214. Off B4090 3 miles (5 km) east of Droitwich. National Trust.
Open: late March to end of October, Saturday to Monday afternoons; also Tuesday and Wednesday afternoons in August.

Hanbury was the home of the Vernon family from Tudor times. The present building was completed by Thomas Vernon in 1701 and is a fine red-brick William and Mary house surmounted by an impressive clock-tower and weathervane. The entrance hall is most dramatic with murals up the stairs depicting the legend of Hercules. These were painted by Sir James Thornhill, best known for his work in the Painted Hall at the Royal Naval Hospital, Greenwich, and the frescoes in the dome of St Paul's Cathedral. Further paintings by him are in the dining room.

Other rooms to see include the parlour, with the Watney Collection of porcelain, the library, the long gallery (78 feet, 24 metres), a number of bedrooms and the Gothick corridors. The orangery was completed about 1735.

A view of Hanbury Hall across the lily pond (left) and the gazebo in the gardens (right).

Hartlebury Castle contains the palace of the Bishops of Worcester and the county museum.

Originally there were extensive formal gardens but these were obliterated in 1776. Today the house is surrounded by 25 acres (10 hectares) of gardens (with a well-preserved icehouse) and an extensive deer park of 400 acres (160 hectares), enclosed from the ancient royal forest of Feckenham.

Hartlebury Castle State Rooms, Hartlebury, Kidderminster DY11 7XZ. Telephone: 01299 250410. Off A449 3 miles (5 km) south of Kidderminster.
Open: Easter Monday to early September, first Sunday in month, bank holidays and Wednesday afternoons only.
Hartlebury Castle is not in any sense a military building now: the only obvious reminder of its former function is the curved section of moat along its western side. The manor of Hartlebury has been held by the Bishops of Worcester since *c*.860 but it was not until late in the thirteenth century that their house here was crenellated, the moat was created and fortified walls and towers added. Some two centuries later a gatehouse and drawbridge were built.

In the Civil War the castle was first held by the Royalist William Sandys, then surrendered under siege in 1646. It became a prison for captured Royalists and most of the defences were demolished after the war. The buildings were then returned to the Bishops of Worcester and the castle we see today is the result of successive phases of building during the past three hundred years.

Visitors can see the Great Hall, originally fifteenth-century, replanned and rebuilt in the seventeenth and eighteenth centuries, and the chapel, medieval in structure but completely redone in 1748-50 in Strawberry Hill Gothic style within. Upstairs is the magnificent eighteenth-century Long Library, completed for Bishop Hurd in 1782, with its extensive collection of rare books and views across the remaining part of the moat.

The Hereford and Worcester County Museum (page 87) occupies the north end of the building.

Harvington Hall, Harvington, Kidderminster DY10 4LR. Telephone: 01562 777846. Near junction of A448 and A450, 4 miles (7 km) east of Kidderminster.

Open: March to October, Sundays, Tuesdays, Wednesdays, Thursdays and bank holidays.

The hall sits peacefully on its moated island as it has done for six centuries or more. Approached by a bridge across the moat, it appears to be an Elizabethan red-brick structure of two four-storeyed towers joined by a double-storey range with incredibly tall Tudor chimneys. Nothing indicates the intricate maze of rooms at varying levels the visitor will encounter inside, nor that the brick walls cover a medieval timber-framed building.

A Catholic stronghold, now in the care of the Archdiocese of Birmingham, Harvington was one of a network of great houses where Mass was said in the dangerous times of the sixteenth and seventeenth centuries. There are more priest holes here than in any other house in England.

Among the rooms visitors see are: the Great Chamber; Lady Yates's Room; the Mermaid Passage with the best Elizabethan wall-paintings in Worcestershire; and Dr Dodd's Library with its swinging beam giving access to a priest's hiding place so cunning that it was lost until 1894. Outside are an Elizabethan malthouse and a charming Georgian chapel, recently restored. A licensed restaurant looks out on to the moat and nearby is the Catholic church of St Mary.

Koi Water Gardens, Bridgnorth Road, Shatterford, near Kidderminster. Telephone: 012997 597. On A442 2 miles (3 km) north of Kidderminster. *Open: daily.*

In the wooded gardens lie a series of eight lakes and numerous smaller pools joined by streams; a circular walk starts from the car park. Red, fallow and sika deer roam at will and there are over forty thousand koi carp. This is a sanctuary for birds and a habitat for many wild flowers. The facilities include trout fishing, aviaries and a snack bar.

Kyre Park, Kyre, Tenbury Wells WR15 8RP. Telephone: 01885 410282. Off B4214 4 miles (7 km) south-east of Tenbury Wells. *Open: Easter to October, daily.*

Restoration of this fascinating garden began in January 1994 and is a continuing project. The garden, attributed to 'Capability' Brown, was created in the eighteenth and nineteenth centuries and its focal point is the delightful series of winding lakes and pools which curve round the estate. Visitors follow a serpentine walk which takes in waterfalls, cascades, ancient yews, specimen trees and a delightful landscape. Ferns are liberally planted in the garden and are for sale on the site. The house is mainly twentieth-century with medieval and Georgian remnants. It is

Harvington Hall has more priest holes than any other house in England.

privately owned and not open but refreshments are served in a conservatory overlooking the grounds.

Joined to the house by an unusual passageway is the delightful Norman church of St Mary, which has an early fourteenth-century south chapel and a tower which may be seventeenth-century. Major restoration work has been undertaken. Of particular interest is a medieval wall-painting of a female saint in one window of the south chapel. Beyond the church is a pleasure garden bounded on one side by a huge brick-built tithe barn of Jacobean times and a circular medieval dovecote complete with revolving ladder.

Little Malvern Court, Little Malvern, near Great Malvern WR14 4JN (OS 150: SO 769403). Telephone: 01684 892988. Off A4104 3 miles (5 km) south of Great Malvern.
Open: April to mid July, Wednesday and Thursday afternoons.

In an idyllic setting on the lower slopes of the Malvern Hills, looking across the Worcestershire lowlands, this delightful house is complemented by a beautiful garden and stands next to Little Malvern Priory (page 64), a Benedictine house founded in the first half of the twelfth century. At the Dissolution in the 1530s much of the church and almost all the domestic buildings of the priory were demolished, but the Prior's Hall survived and was incorporated in the later house, Little Malvern Court. The principal feature is the splendid early fourteenth-century roof. Little Malvern Court was one of Worcestershire's Catholic safe houses, having a secret chapel reached by a concealed staircase. There have been considerable alterations, with additional building, from Elizabethan times onwards. Visitors can see the Prior's Hall, including a collection of family and religious paintings and needlework.

The gardens extend to 10 acres (4 hectares) and include the five former fishponds of the priory, which now form a series of ornamental lakes. The great lime tree which dominates the garden is over 250 years old. Queen Victoria is reputed to have played under it in 1831.

The Old Palace, Deansway, Worcester WR1 2JE. Telephone (diocesan offices): 01905 20537.
Open: weekdays only, by appointment only.

Much of the interior is thirteenth-century behind an eighteenth-century façade. There are rib-vaulted undercrofts from the time of Bishop Giffard, around 1275, and the chancel of the chapel remains. Visitors are conducted around a series of rooms.

Pershore College of Horticulture, Avonbank, Pershore WR10 3JP. Telephone: 01386 552443. On A44 1 mile (2 km) east of Pershore.
Open: daily.

This is England's only specialist college of horticulture, appropriately located in the Vale of Evesham. The main building, Avonbank, is early nineteenth-century and was originally the house for the Wyke Estate. During the Second World War it was used as a hostel for the Women's Land Army. As it is a large working college, areas of ground coverage are constantly changing and new points of interest being developed. Among the areas to be seen are the gardens, arboretum, orchards, glasshouses, rose gardens and container beds. There is an excellent plant centre including a tropical house.

The Priory, Kemerton, near Tewkesbury GL20 7JN (OS 150: SO 950379). Telephone: 01386 725258. On minor road 10 miles (16 km) south-west of Evesham.
Open (garden only): June to September, Friday afternoons and some Sundays.

This 4 acre (1.5 hectare) garden is situated on the lower south-facing slope of Bredon Hill. It features long herbaceous borders planted in colour groups, a sunken garden and a number of themed areas separated by hedges and walls. One wall of the former Kemerton Priory is preserved as a garden feature. Bredon Hill provides an attractive backdrop to views of the garden.

Spetchley Park, Spetchley, Worcester WR5 1RS. Telephone: 01905 345213 or 345224. On A422 3 miles (5 km) east of Worcester.
Open (grounds only): April to September,

The ornamental bridge in Spetchley Park.

Tuesdays to Fridays and bank holiday Mondays, and also Sunday afternoons.

The grounds extend to some 30 acres (12 hectares) and provide a number of varied walks for visitors through formal enclosed gardens, wooded areas with superb specimen trees, and wide expanses of lawn leading down to the lake. There are red and fallow deer in the neighbouring park. A moat crossed by an attractive footbridge flows into the lake and there are a number of conservatories and a root house with a conical thatched roof.

The house (not open) is the home of the Berkeley family and was built in the early nineteenth century. See also Berkeley's Hospital (page 72) and Spetchley church (page 68).

Stone House Cottage Garden, Stone, Kidderminster DY10 4BG (OS 139: SO 862749). Telephone: 01562 69902. Approached along side road off A448, 3 miles (5 km) east of Kidderminster.
Open: early March to end of October, Wednesday to Saturday; extra opening in May and June.

This pleasant, mostly walled garden features towers around the walls, giving pano-

ramic views over it. The thick hedges divide the garden into a succession of outdoor rooms, each with its own colours and fragrances. There is an excellent collection of rare and unusual wall shrubs and climbers. There is a nursery and plant sales area adjacent to the garden.

White Cottage Garden, Earls Common Road, Stock Green, Redditch B96 6SZ. Telephone: 01386 792414. Off A422 Worcester to Alcester road at Dormston.
Open: early April to early October. Closed Wednesdays, Thursdays and alternate Sundays.

This is a 2 acre (0.8 hectare) garden with large herbaceous and shrub borders containing numerous unusual varieties and a specialist collection of hardy geraniums. There is a stream and a natural garden area contains cowslips, primroses and other wild flowers. A nursery sells plants propagated from the garden.

Witley Court and Grounds, Great Witley WR6 6JT. Telephone: 01299 896636. Approached by an unmade road off A443. English Heritage.

Open: throughout the year, but closed on Mondays and Tuesdays from November to April.

One of England's most extensive and extraordinary great house ruins, Witley Court is haunted by the ghosts of its opulent Victorian heyday. Between 1859 and 1861 the first Earl of Dudley created here what could more appropriately be regarded as a palace rather than a country house. Everything was on a huge scale: the house, the gardens and the fountains – a fitting setting for the sumptuous entertainment dispensed for Victorian royalty and aristocracy. Ownership eventually passed to Sir Herbert Smith, a Kidderminster blanket tycoon, but disaster struck in 1937 when fire devastated part of the building. Abandoned for many years, it was in danger of demolition but has fortunately now been taken into the care of English Heritage.

The gardens have gone, but the Poseidon Fountain with its huge prancing horse is under restoration and is returning to something like its former glory. Visitors wishing to understand the full fascinating story of this great house are recommended to study the literature available in the English Heritage shop on site. Adjacent to the house is the incredible baroque church of St Michael (page 61).

Worcester Guildhall, High Street, Worcester. Telephone: 01905 723471.
Open: daily.

Worcester's Guildhall is an impressive, regularly proportioned building extending some distance along the narrow pedestrianised High Street. To fully appreciate its exterior, one needs initially to stand on the opposite side of the street for a view that encompasses both the lofty central building (1721) and the flanking wings (1725 and 1727). Cross then to stand inside the iron railings, made in Robert Bakewell's Derbyshire foundry, to enjoy the exuberant central bay. The front door is flanked by apses containing statues of Charles I and Charles II. Look carefully for their adversary Oliver Cromwell: wickedly caricatured in a gargoyle-like head, he occupies the keystone above the fanlight, nailed up by the ears! Queen Anne, who died a few years before the Guildhall's construction, occupies another apse in the second storey of the façade. Above that is the superbly ornate semicircular device with the royal arms, and

The ruins of Witley Court are now in the care of English Heritage.

Eastgrove Cottage Garden.

Little Malvern Court gardens.

Worcester Guildhall.

Labour, Peace, Justice, Plenty and Chastisement represented along the parapet, interspersed with urns. Thomas White, a highly accomplished local stonemason, designed the building and cut much of the stonework.

Inside there are two large assembly rooms occupying the whole width of the building. The ground-floor room has an interesting collection of ancient fire buckets and large portraits of civic dignitaries. Climb the stairs, lined with more portraits, to one of Worcester's great treasures, the magnificent Assembly Room. Three huge chandeliers hang from the ornately painted ceiling and on the walls there are large portraits of county dignitaries, and also one of Queen Victoria by William Skelton and two of George III, one commemorating his visit to Worcester in 1788.

Refreshments are served in the Assembly Room in the visitor season. The tourist information centre is located in the south wing of the building.

7
Museums

Bewdley

Bewdley Museum, The Shambles, Load Street, Bewdley DY12 2AE. Telephone: 01299 403573.

Open: March to November, Mondays to Saturdays, also Sunday afternoons.

Bewdley's neo-classical town hall of 1808 hides the entrance to a unique museum, occupying what used to be a whole street of butchers' premises. Each archway now holds either a display or a craft workshop. The aim of the museum is to explain the numerous crafts and industries once thriving in and around the town. Two factors were dominant: the Wyre Forest and the river Severn. Charcoal burning survived until the 1950s and this is featured along with various types of sawing techniques and wood-using crafts such as wheelwrighting and coopering. Coracles were commonly used on the Severn and there is an annual coracle-making workshop.

Running parallel to the Shambles is a renovated brass foundry. Here visitors can see a series of rooms reconstructing the various processes of brassmaking which ended in Bewdley in the 1960s after 250 years of production. The museum also includes a number of outdoor areas and there are displays of ropemaking, clay-pipe making and various other events regularly throughout the year.

Broadway

Broadway Teddy Bear Museum, 76 High Street, Broadway WR12 7AJ. Telephone: 01386 858323.

Open: daily.

The front of this delightful museum is a bear, doll and general nostalgia shop and through a door at the rear of the shop is a world of everlasting childhood. Here are hundreds of bears, dolls and innumerable other toys. The legendary Steiff bears are well represented as well as superb examples of early Farnell, Merrythought, Chad Valley and other

bears from England and all over the world. The hall of fame showcase introduces bears with a story: Paddington arriving at the station, Hundred Acre Wood with Pooh and his friends, and Goldilocks disturbed by the Three Bears. Famous bear artists have contributed to the *Alice in Wonderland* scenes and visitors will meet bears that have been rescued or donated to the museum. Broadway Bear lives in the museum and delightful scenes are depicted as visitors are taken by him through the seasons in the Cotswolds.

The Shambles at Bewdley Museum.

Wagon ride at Avoncroft Museum of Historic Buildings.

A merchant's house from Bromsgrove was Avoncroft Museum's first exhibit.

A reconstruction of salt extraction at Droitwich Heritage Centre.

Bromsgrove

Avoncroft Museum of Historic Buildings, Stoke Heath, Bromsgrove B60 4JR. Telephone: 01527 831886.

Open: June, July and August, daily; April, May, September and October, daily except Mondays; March and November, daily except Mondays and Fridays.

Located on a 15 acre (6 hectare) site on the southern outskirts of Bromsgrove, this museum has over twenty preserved buildings in pleasant spacious grounds. The primary aim of the museum, opened in 1967, is to save important vernacular buildings from destruction and the collection, drawn from Worcestershire and neighbouring counties, continues to grow. The exhibits include traditional agricultural buildings, industrial workshops for nailmaking and chainmaking, and furnished houses, including a prefab dismantled only in 1980. There is a working windmill producing stoneground flour for sale.

In 1991 the opening of a new large hall for concerts and other events brought a major project to fruition. The hall is covered by the fourteenth-century beamed roof from the now ruined Guesten Hall in the precincts of Worcester Cathedral.

A project on an entirely different scale was opened in 1994: the BT National Telephone Kiosk Collection, which is accommodated in a specially designed urban environment behind the shop.

Children enjoy this museum. There is a programme of special events and demonstrations throughout the year and goats, geese and poultry wander happily between the buildings. As well as the shop, there are a refreshment bar, picnic and play areas and an educational centre.

Bromsgrove Museum, 26 Birmingham Road, Bromsgrove B61 0DD. Telephone: 01527 577983.

Open: Mondays to Saturdays, and Sunday afternoons.

The museum is accommodated in the renovated coach-house of the Georgian Davenal House next door, opposite a car park which makes a convenient starting point for a walk around the town centre (page 16).

There is an entertaining street layout with shops such as a gramophone and wireless shop, a ladies' hairdresser, a shoe shop, a toy shop and a cobbler, among others. Each shop window is full of goods available around 1900. Bromsgrove's traditional industries are featured and explained: making nails, glass and buttons. Of particular interest is the display of the Bromsgrove Guild, founded by Walter Gilbert at the end of the nineteenth century. It was the largest guild of decorative artists in Britain, specialising in stained glass, ornamental plasterwork and wood carving. The Guild achieved national fame and a royal warrant for the gates of Buckingham Palace and international recognition for the huge rose window of Montreal Cathedral and forty stained glass windows in Johannesburg Cathedral. The Guild's original premises can still be seen in Station Road, Bromsgrove.

Droitwich

Droitwich Spa Heritage Centre, St Richard's House, Victoria Square, Droitwich WR9 8DS. Telephone: 01905 774312.
Open: daily except Sundays.

The Heritage Centre occupies the ground floor of the former reception building for the Brine Baths, built in the 1880s and closed in 1975. Modernised baths are now located behind this building as part of a private hospital.

A series of imaginative and informative displays explains the geological reasons why salt is found under Droitwich, the history of salt extraction through the centuries and the social history of Droitwich. Labour in the salt-processing works was extremely exhausting: the heat was so great that men worked almost naked. The development of Droitwich as a spa is recorded in a display of old photographs.

In a separate room is the 'Droitwich Calling' exhibition, an evocation of the early decades of broadcasting, when Droitwich appeared on all wireless dials. A further room is used for a variety of temporary exhibitions and the foyer houses an award-winning tourist information centre.

Evesham

The Almonry Heritage Centre, Abbey Gate, Evesham WR11 4BG. Telephone: 01386 446944.

Open: Mondays to Saturdays, including bank holidays, and Sunday afternoons (also Sunday mornings in August). Closed mid December to early January.

The Almonry was part of the monastic buildings of the abbey, the offices of the almoner, the monk whose duty it was to distribute alms and organise assistance for the local sick and poor. The earliest parts of the building date from around 1400, when the monastery was a powerful and thriving community. Some of the building is timber-framed, some stone-built. Its construction can be seen from the front, before entering, from the garden at the rear, and inside the various rooms. In the panelled Simon de Montfort Room there is a relief model of the battle of Evesham in 1265 (see pages 9 and 25). The Abbey Room has a large stone fireplace with five quatrefoil decorations in the lintel. Four of these bear designs which commemorate the wedding of Prince Arthur to Catherine of Aragon. This room contains a detailed model of the abbey buildings and shows how the great complex looked in its heyday. There is also a superb mahogany font of 1793.

Among other displays are: lace and sewing; wireless, television and telephone equipment; the home front in the Second World War; a Victorian bedroom; law and order; Evesham's charters. To the rear is a delightful walled garden which houses yet more exhibits.

Great Malvern

Malvern Museum, Abbey Gateway, Abbey Road, Great Malvern WR14 3ES. Telephone: 01684 567811.
Open: Easter to end of October, daily, except Wednesdays in school terms.

This small but well-presented museum, housed in the second oldest building in Malvern, depicts the town's history from pre-medieval to modern times, with facts and artefacts to delight all ages. Of particular interest are the rocks and fossils in the geology room and the four rooms upstairs covering Malvern's early history, the water cure which made the town famous, the Victorian era and the modern development of the radar establishment. Car enthusiasts will enjoy the setion on Morgan cars, still being made locally. Next to the museum is a Perpendicular Gothic town house with a delightful butcher's shop front of around 1900.

Hartlebury

Hereford and Worcester County Museum, Hartlebury Castle, Hartlebury, Kidderminster DY11 7XZ. Telephone: 01299 250416. On B4193 3 miles (5 km) south of Kidderminster. *Open: March to November, Monday to Thursday, also Friday and Sunday afternoons. Closed Saturdays and Good Friday.*

Housed in the north wing of the Bishop's palace at Hartlebury Castle (page 76), the museum displays the social, cultural and economic life of the county over the centuries. The three-storey building contains fourteen display areas, a number being presented as room settings. The former kitchen of the castle was located in this wing, and it has been renovated to accommodate a display of utensils spanning more than three centuries. Other rooms are used to display many of the items from the museum's extensive costume and furniture collections. A panelled seventeenth-century room, a Georgian parlour and a Victorian drawing room display the earlier collections; further groups cover the changes in

women's fashions up to the First World War. A reconstructed Victorian nursery illustrates the lives of the younger members of the household and their mentors, the nursemaid and the nursery governess. Among other collections are an extensive display of toys; a medical gallery with surgical instruments, cases and medical books; and examples of the work of the Bromsgrove Guild (page 86).

In the courtyard and nearby buildings there are a Victorian laundry, a restored cider mill and a large collection of horse-drawn carriages, including beautiful restored gypsy caravans.

Kidderminster

Kidderminster Railway Museum, Station Approach, Comberton Hill, Kidderminster DY10 1QX. Telephone: 01562 825316. *Open: when trains are running on the Severn Valley Railway (see page 101).*

This award-winning museum is housed in a former Great Western Railway grain and wool store of 1878, rescued from dereliction by the volunteers who run the museum. The ground floor of the building has an extensive and fascinating collection of railway memorabilia: lamps, signs, telegraph and signal equipment and hundreds of other treas-

Bordesley Abbey Visitor Centre, Redditch, displays finds from the excavations.

The Elgar Birthplace Museum at Lower Broadheath.

cures. A platform in one corner has a row of working signal levers for would-be signalmen of all ages to use.

The upper floor, with beautifully renovated floorboards, is used for displays, conferences, art exhibitions and the like. A library and archive room has been created at one end, using window frames rescued from a warehouse at Gloucester: the cast-iron bosses at the junction of each set of panes have been painstakingly painted in contrasting colours. On the wall is a splendid half-case clock originally in use at Dava station on the Aviemore line.

A sales area and refreshment bar downstairs help to provide funds for the museum. Immediately beside the museum is the Kidderminster terminus of the Severn Valley Railway.

Lower Broadheath

Elgar Birthplace Museum, Lower Broadheath, near Worcester (OS 150: SO 806557). Telephone: 01905 333224. Off A44

3 miles (5 km) west of Worcester.
Open: daily except Wednesdays; afternoons only from October to April; closed altogether mid January to mid February.

This pleasant red-brick country cottage represented Elgar's spiritual home throughout his life: when, at seventy-four, a baronetcy was conferred on him by George V, he took the title Sir Edward Elgar, first Baronet of Broadheath. The cottage and its neighbouring countryside provided the inspiration for much of Elgar's most happy and relaxed compositions.

Among childhood items displayed are his birth certificate, some early photographs and a child's drum. Probably the most interesting exhibit is Elgar's desk, laid out as he would have wished, with his reading glasses, quill, pens and cigar, cigarette and snuff boxes. There is the superb silver casket presented to him when the Freedom of Worcester was conferred on him in 1905 and display cabinets full of honours from Britain and abroad. There is also a collection of original scores

The river Severn and the Glover's Needle spire at Worcester.

Forge Mill Needle Museum at Redditch.

and many other memorabilia.

An Elgar Trail (page 104) is signposted around the local countryside that was his inspiration.

Redditch

Bordesley Abbey Visitor Centre, Needle Mill Lane, Riverside, Redditch B97 6RR. Telephone: 01527 62509. At the extreme northern edge of Redditch, off A441.
Open: April to September, daily except Fridays; afternoons only on Saturdays and Sundays. Reduced opening times in winter.

The excellent purpose-built centre displays finds from archaeological excavations and describes the daily life of Bordesley Abbey. An upstairs window gives a panoramic view of the site and accompanying panels explain the layout of the buildings. Bordesley Abbey was a Cistercian house founded by Empress Maud in 1138. Substantial efforts were necessary to enable the site to be used for building: the river Arrow had to be diverted and the marshy valley floor drained to provide adequate foundations.

The abbey was demolished at the Dissolution in 1538. Archaeological excavations have gone on here since 1969 and the first investigations were undertaken as long ago as 1864.

The Centre has two floors of informative displays and includes a shop, education wing and cloistered picnic area. It shares its site with the Forge Mill Needle Museum.

Forge Mill Needle Museum, Needle Mill Lane, Riverside, Redditch B97 6RR. Telephone: 01527 62509. At the extreme northern edge of Redditch, off A441.
Open: April to September, daily except Fridays; afternoons only on Saturdays and Sundays. Reduced opening times in winter.

At the beginning of the twentieth century Redditch was the needlemaking capital of the world with an output of some seventy million needles per week from the district. Forge Mill, a two-storey watermill, was partly working up to 1958 and visitors can see much of the equipment and machinery still in place. There are also interesting displays of needles, fishing tackle and associated products.

Tenbury Wells

Tenbury Museum, Goff's School, Cross Street, Tenbury Wells. Telephone: 01584 811669.
Open: May to September, Tuesdays, Saturdays and Sundays.

Tenbury's brief period of fame as a spa resort is recorded here along with a wide variety of exhibits on the social and agricultural life of the district. Hop growing is especially important here in the Teme valley. The work of Dr Henry Hickman is featured: he was a pioneer of research into anaesthesia in the early nineteenth century.

Upton upon Severn

Upton Heritage Centre, The Pepperpot, Upton upon Severn. Telephone: 01684 594200.
Open: Easter to Spring Bank Holiday, weekends only; Spring Bank Holiday to end of September, daily.

Located in the restored bell-tower of the medieval church and surrounded by a pleasant garden area, the centre tells the story of Upton as an important centre for river Severn navigation over the centuries. There is a special feature on the Civil War engagement of 1651.

Worcester

The Commandery Civil War Centre, Sidbury, Worcester WR1 2HU. Telephone: 01905 355071.
Open: Mondays to Saturdays, also Sunday afternoons.

This is England's only museum devoted entirely to explaining the Civil War (1642-51) and particularly to the battle of Worcester in 1651. Worcester's prominent role in the conflict is described in Chapter 1. The early history of this site is obscure. It was known as the Hospital of St Wulstan and the earliest dated reference is 1221. The name 'Commandery' first appears towards the end of the thirteenth century.

The Commandery is a complex of buildings located where Sidbury, the main southern exit from Worcester, passes over the Worcester & Birmingham Canal. There are late fifteenth-century timber-framed and later brick buildings grouped around a delightful courtyard and gardens. The Commandery would be worth visiting for the superbly restored buildings alone, apart from the imaginative interpretation of the Civil War. The most significant room is the Painted Chamber, which contains several wall-paintings from around 1500.

In a whole series of rooms on both the ground and first floors in two ranges of buildings audio-visual techniques and wax tableaux are used to recount the background, main events and local significance of the Civil War. The shop stocks several useful leaflets and publications, including one on a Civil War trail.

Outside, the Commandery is fronted by a long quayside and lock, and there is a pleasant tearoom with outdoor seating on the quay. This is a wholly delightful experience, not to be missed.

Royal Worcester Porcelain and Museum of Worcester Porcelain, Severn Street, Worcester WR1 2NE. Telephone: 01905 23221.
Open: Mondays to Saturdays.

The museum contains the world's largest collection of Worcester porcelain arranged chronologically to span two and a half centuries of production since the company's foundation in 1751. A company museum was originally founded in 1879 by Richard Binns (1819-1900), the company's art director and historian. His principal aim was to educate and inspire the company workforce with examples of early Worcester ware and other artworks. The collection was also available for public viewing.

In the 1930s this original museum and the Royal Worcester company were acquired by Charles Dyson Perrins and in 1946 he created a trust to administer jointly his personal collection and the company museum collection. These collections were first exhibited together in 1951 to mark the company's bicentenary, the exhibition being opened by the then Princess Elizabeth.

The Commandery Civil War Centre and the Worcester & Birmingham Canal at Worcester.

Worcester porcelain began with a secret recipe in 1751. It is interesting to reflect that the wonderful collection in the museum, and the building housing it, derive largely from wealth created by another secret recipe: for Lea & Perrins Worcestershire sauce. The history of Worcester porcelain is described in chapter 11.

Other attractions here are the factory shop, the seconds shop, a tearoom and factory tours (prior booking advisable).

Tudor House Museum, Friar Street, Worcester WR1 2NA. Telephone: 01905 20904.
Open: daily except Thursdays and Sundays.

Housed in a prime example of a timber-framed town house and courtyard, in one of the oldest streets in Worcester's city centre, this delightful museum illustrates the social history of Worcester through the ages. Tudor House is some five hundred years old and has been home and workplace to a weaver, a salter and a barber. Part of it was formerly a tavern, the Cross Keys, and it was also a coffee house and, later, a school clinic and dentist's surgery. Bygone eras are evoked by a series of room sets: a Victorian kitchen, an Edwardian schoolroom, a 1920s office, wartime Worcester, and so on. Hundreds of everyday objects from homes, workplaces and shops are crowded into still more rooms creating an informal and pleasantly nostalgic atmosphere.

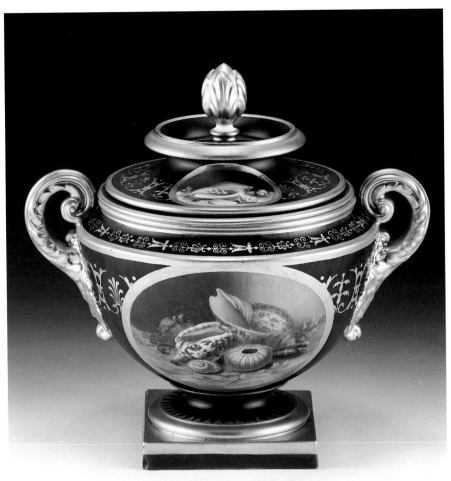

One of a pair of Worcester porcelain ice pails, made c.1815, and now exhibited in the Museum of Worcester Porcelain, Worcester.

Worcester City Museum, Art Gallery and Library, Foregate Street, Worcester WR1 1DT. Telephone: 01905 25371.
Open: Mondays to Wednesdays, Fridays and Saturdays. Closed Thursdays and Sundays, Good Friday and Christmas period.

The museum occupies the Victorian Institute, built to commemorate the Diamond Jubilee of Queen Victoria, a typical piece of confident, height of the Empire architecture with a red terracotta façade and Dutch gables. Inside, an impressive staircase with sturdy balustrade and columns leads up to the first-floor museum and art gallery.

The permanent collection of the gallery has some good nineteenth-century work: watercolours by David Cox, Welsh landscapes by B. W. Leader and representative works by Laura Knight, Blandford Fletcher and Peter de Wint among others. The large and lively 'Market Day' by Frank Calderon is likely to give pleasure, as is the splendid 'Snow on the Malverns', which hangs on the staircase wall. Items from the permanent collection are not always on show: the gallery has a policy of mounting frequent travelling exhibitions of modern art.

Of particular interest are the large gallery and annexe devoted to the Worcestershire Regiment, now amalgamated with the Sherwood Foresters. The regiment won nine Victoria Crosses in the First World War and there is an impressive collection of colours, uniforms, drums and other memorabilia. There is a Japanese field gun captured at Kohima, where the advance against India was halted in the Second World War.

The museum shop is in the foyer and the pleasant balcony café on the first floor. The library on the ground floor has a well-stocked section of local reference books.

8
Industrial archaeology

Canals

Worcestershire has two main canals, the Worcester & Birmingham and the Staffordshire & Worcestershire, which remain open and busy with pleasure craft in the summer season. They provide numerous locations for investigating industrial archaeology, often in delightful surroundings. Another canal linked Droitwich to the Severn and to the Worcester & Birmingham Canal.

Droitwich Canals, river Severn to Hanbury Junction (OS 150).

Droitwich Barge Canal (opened 1771) connects Droitwich with the river Severn and is 5¹/2 miles (10 km) long. Droitwich Junction Canal (opened 1854) linked the Barge Canal with the Worcester & Birmingham Canal at Hanbury Wharf (OS 150: SO 922620) on the B4090, a distance of 1¹/2 miles (3 km).

The Barge Canal was built to facilitate export of salt from Droitwich via the river Severn and its associated waterways. Coal to fire the brine-boiling furnaces was the main import. A link eastwards to the Worcester & Birmingham Canal (fully opened in 1815) was available along the small river Salwarpe but this was tortuous and unreliable: hence the Droitwich Junction Canal was opened in 1854. By this time, however, the railways were already beginning to divert bulk traffic from the canal system. When John Corbett (page 103) built the new salt-processing works at Stoke Prior on the Worcester & Birmingham Canal much of the remaining trade on the Droitwich Canals inevitably disappeared. The canals were finally abandoned in 1949 but a thriving trust has renovated much of the canal and the associated bridges and locks. A towpath runs the length of the Barge Canal. Access points include Vines Park (Droitwich), Salwarpe church and Hanbury Junction.

Staffordshire & Worcestershire Canal, Stourport to Great Haywood (OS 138).

Opened fully in 1772, the total length is 46¹/2 miles (75 km), with 15 miles (24 km) in Worcestershire. It was engineered by James Brindley to join the Trent & Mersey Canal with the river Severn. The junction was originally planned for the existing river port at Bewdley but the town fathers would have none of it. Brindley diverted his route to the Stour valley and a new town, Stourport (page 36), was born at its confluence with the Severn. The canal was a great success commercially and Stourport became a thriving inland port.

Stourport Basins (OS 138: SO 710810). The basin area is a magnet for canal enthusiasts and sightseers: a wide variety of craft are always moored here. Locks lift craft up from the Severn to a basin area surrounded by buildings of the canal era, notably the Tontine Hotel (1788), opened by the canal company, and the adjacent hop merchants' houses and the long main warehouse with its clock-tower. From here the towpath leads through Stourport, past a derelict warehouse and wharf area and a canalside inn. It is possible to continue walking north along the Stour valley for 5 miles (8 km) to Kidderminster and beyond for the whole length of the canal.

Kidderminster (OS 138). There are numerous access points to the towpath and the premises of several carpet factories and other industrial concerns line the canal. In the nineteenth century Kidderminster was the leading carpet-manufacturing town in the world. The industry remains important today, although the town's industrial base has widened greatly. As long ago as the thirteenth century, Flemish weavers laid the foundations of the town's pre-eminence in heavy textile weaving. Carpets developed as a cottage industry and in the early eighteenth century John Broom, a persistent entrepreneur, made and lost three fortunes improving hand looms to develop

The Severn Valley Railway at Upper Arley.

Stourport Canal Basin and the early nineteenth-century dock warehouse.

carpet weaving; the first factory opened in the mid 1730s. Luddism reared its head in 1828 when power looms began to threaten many weavers' jobs, but in the subsequent decades Kidderminster attained unrivalled stature in carpet manufacturing.

There is a particularly pleasant canalside spot just below St Mary's church (page 63). North of the town the canal passes through two further Worcestershire villages: Wolverley (page 39) and Cookley, where it tunnels under the village, before entering neighbouring Staffordshire.

The Worcester & Birmingham Canal,
Worcester to Birmingham (OS 139 and 150).

Opened fully in 1815, the total length is 30 miles (48 km), of which about 25 miles (40 km) are in Worcestershire. Some of the more interesting sites on the canal are described here, moving from Worcester towards Birmingham.

Diglis Locks and Basin, Worcester (OS 150: SO 850539). Two locks 76 feet (23 metres) long raise ships from the river Severn to the basin level. The basin is an interesting place with buildings of the canal era and a wide variety of craft. Dredging allowed ships of up to 400 tonnes to be accommodated after 1890. The timber trade is much in evidence here and an oil-storage depot was built in 1929. A canalside walk runs right through the city (page 44): it is possible, with only minor deviations, to walk all the way to Birmingham.

Tibberton Bridge (OS 150: SO 905581). Near Tibberton there is a wharf area, with riverside parking and an inn.

Hanbury Junction (OS 150: SO 922630). On the B4090 east of Droitwich, where the canal joins the Droitwich Canal (see below), are a canalside inn and other buildings.

Stoke Works (OS 150: SO 940667). This was the site of the salt works of John Corbett (page 103), now a chemical factory. There are canalside buildings, including an inn with a terrace, and a picnic area.

Stoke Wharf (OS 150: SO 951670). Here, on the B4091, there are a number of canalside commercial buildings, a wharf area and an inn.

Stoke Pound (OS 150: SO 962679). This delightful hamlet has two canal bridges and an inn. Just along the towpath is the lowest of the Tardebigge flight of locks.

Tardebigge Locks and Wharf (OS 139: SO 997694). Off A448, the flight of locks is one of the wonders of canal engineering in Great Britain: thirty locks in 2½ miles (4 km) lift the canal on to the Midlands plateau. In all the canal has had to climb fifty-six locks since Diglis Basin, a rise of some 400 feet (112 metres). A large wharf area has some delightful cottages at the top of the flight and is a busy place in summer. From a hilltop the splendid Tardebigge church (page 69) looks down. Northwards the canal disappears into a tunnel, to reappear on the outskirts of Birmingham.

Metalworking
Avoncroft Museum of Historic Buildings,
Stoke Heath, Bromsgrove B60 4JR. Telephone: 01527 831886.
Open: June, July and August, daily; April, May, September and October, daily except Mondays; March and November, daily except Mondays and Fridays.

The museum is described in detail in chapter 7 but two buildings here recreate conditions in the metal-processing industry in the nineteenth century. The nailshop is typical of many that were formerly found in north Worcestershire and up into the Black Country. These were often small-scale, family-run businesses, adjacent to the family home, employing both men and women.

The chainshop is an example of factory-type production with a line of hearths and accompanying anvils. Chain production was also organised as a cottage industry. Again, both sexes worked in the industry, women being responsible for manufacturing the smaller-gauge chains. The example shown at Avoncroft was in regular use for chain production until 1969.

The museum has a calendar of special events throughout each year. These include chainmaking, blacksmithing, racksawing and other traditional manufacturing skills.

Churchill Forge, Churchill (OS 139: SO 884796). 6 miles (10 km) north-east of Kidderminster, along a minor road off A456.

The forge building stands beside the dammed-up pool in Churchill village. The building is in the care of a trust who are renovating it but visitors can view it, including its two waterwheels, from the public footpath beside the pool. Records of a forge here go back to the thirteenth century: production ceased only in the mid 1970s. The forge used to produce edge tools – spades, hooks and so on – for agriculture and gardening.

Forge Mill Needle Museum, Needle Mill Lane, Riverside, Redditch B97 6RR. Telephone: 01527 62509.

The museum features another of the industries which made the West Midlands the world's leading metal-processing and manufacturing region in the nineteenth century. It is described on page 90.

Railways

Lickey Incline, Bromsgrove (OS 139: SO 983710). Parallel to a minor road off B4096 near the village of Burcot 3 miles (5 km) north-east of Bromsgrove.

This is the steepest railway gradient in England (1 in 37.7) and used to cause steam locomotives to emit great clouds of smoke when climbing it. One engine exploded in 1840 and the engineers were killed. Their tombstones are in Bromsgrove churchyard (page 18). The steep climb up on to the Birmingham plateau is the same feature that necessitated the Tardebigge lock flight (page 97) on the Worcester & Birmingham Canal 2 miles (3 km) to the south.

Severn Valley Railway. See page 101.

Worcester's industries

Four locations represent the main traditional industries of the city: glovemaking, engineering, saucemaking and porcelain manufacture.

Fownes Hotel, City Walls Road, Worcester (OS 150: SO 855545).

Another canalside location, this luxury hotel

The tombs of engineers killed on the Lickey Incline are in the churchyard at Bromsgrove.

The present Fownes Hotel in Worcester was once a glovemaking factory.

occupies the converted and extended main factory building of the former Fownes glovemaking company. Fownes originated in Battersea, London, in 1777. John Fownes subsequently moved to Worcester and in 1882, when the company was employing one thousand people, the present factory building was constructed. The glove industry declined and production was transferred to Warminster, Wiltshire, leaving the factory empty. The three-storey building is a prominent feature of the canalside landscape. Inside are pictures of the various glovemaking processes set in the places where the work was originally undertaken. Across the canal in the Commandery Civil War Centre is a recreation of a Fownes craftsman at work.

Heenan & Froude Engineering Works, Worcester (OS 150: SO 855553). At the junction of Shrub Hill Road and Tolladine Road, near the Worcester & Birmingham Canal.

The canal brought the necessary raw materials to establish heavy engineering in Worcester. This building is a prime example of Victorian large-scale factory construction.

Lea & Perrins Factory, Midland Road, Worcester (OS 150: SO 859547).

The world-famous Worcestershire sauce was originally made in 1836, in a chemist shop in Broad Street, in the city centre. In 1896 a new factory was constructed in Midland Road, alongside the main railway line. The main building is a large square, with the central courtyard glassed over. A second storey was added in 1912. The building has a plain symmetrical façade with a central archway constructed for horse-drawn wagons. The fine four-faced clock which surmounts the building is a well-known feature. The railside location emphasises the dominance of railways for transport by the late nineteenth century.

Royal Worcester Porcelain, Severn Street, Worcester WR1 2NE (OS 150: SO 852544). Telephone: 01905 23221.

A number of industrial buildings of varying ages can be seen here, as well as the Museum of Worcester Porcelain. This is also a canalside area, emphasising the important effect that transport had on industrial location and development. See also pages 91 and 107.

9
Other places to visit

Annard Woollen Mill, Handgate Farm, Church Lench (OS 150: SP 026497). Telephone: 01386 870270. Off A435 4 miles (7 km) north of Evesham.
Open: Thursdays to Sundays and bank holidays.

A wide range of mohairs and wools are sold here together with tweeds, silks and skirt lengths. There is an old sixteen-spindle Ayrton ball-winding machine which can be operated for visitors. A small herd of mohair goats is kept on the farm.

Astley Vineyards, Astley, Stourport-on-Severn DY13 0RU (OS 138: SO 805671). Telephone: 01299 822907. 3 miles (5 km) south of Stourport, off B4196.
Open: daily.

This award-winning vineyard lies in an area where Benedictine monks made wine in the thirteenth century. The shop provides tastings and visitors can see the 5 acre (2 hectare) vineyard where four types of grapes are grown.

Barnfield Cider Mill, Broadway Road, Broadway (OS 150: SP 084383). Telephone: 01386 853145. 2 miles (3 km) north-west of Broadway village.
Open: daily.

Visitors wishing to acquire some of the local tipples of the Vale of Evesham will find a good selection here. There are ciders and perry made from the local apples and pears, and a range of wines made from local plums, strawberries and rasberries. Non-alcoholic drinks include ginger beer and elderflower cordial. A display of cidermaking through the ages includes a Paris wine press of the 1920s, and a stone mill with wooden presses and scratter (pulping machine).

Beckford Silk Printing Centre, Ashton Road, Beckford GL20 7AD. Telephone: 01386 881507. Off A435 6 miles (10 km) south-west of Evesham.
Open: daily except Sunday.

Silk ties, scarves, blouses and waistcoats are among the brightly coloured exclusive designs available here. The printshop and most working areas are open to the public and visitors can see hand printing in progress. The retail shop has a wide range of the company's products including some seconds. There is a licensed coffee shop.

Bennett's Farm Park, Malvern Road, Worcester (OS 150: SO 838527). Telephone: 01905 748102. Near junction of A422 and A449 on extreme south-west edge of Worcester.
Open: Easter to end of August, daily.

The farm site overlooks the broad meadows bordering the river Teme. It is a working farm, with animals to feed, a nature trail, fishing lake and play area. There is a museum of old farm machinery, a teashop and a shop. At milking time there are guided tours of the milking areas.

Domestic Fowl Trust, Honeybourne Pastures, Honeybourne, Evesham WR11 5QJ. Telephone: 01386 833083. Off B4035 5 miles (8 km) east of Evesham.
Open: daily except Fridays.

This international collection includes 150 breeds of domestic ducks, geese, hens, turkeys and pheasants. Attractions also include a children's farm, adventure playground, gift shop and tearoom.

Dunstall Castle Folly, Dunstall Common (OS 150: SO 886428). 4 miles (7 km) north-east of Upton upon Severn, on minor road through Earl's Croome off A4104.
Open: at any time.

This mock Norman castle ruin is ascribed to Sanderson Miller (1717-80), the architect of Hagley Hall. Like Broadway Tower, it was a folly on the formerly extensive Croome Estate of the Coventry family. The structure consists of two round towers joined by an archway and a square tower set at an angle connected by a further arch.

The Falconry Centre (Hagley), Hurrans Garden Centre, Kidderminster Road South, Hagley DY9 0JB. Telephone: 01562 700014. On A456 5 miles (8 km) north-east of Kidderminster.
Open: daily.
Over 120 birds of prey – owls, hawks, falcons and eagles – are accommodated here on an extensive site surrounded by conifers and poplars. Facilities include a demonstration area, souvenir shop and picnic area. Residential courses on falconry are available. Other attractions include a pets' corner and cage-bird aviaries and shop.

Jinney Ring Craft Centre, Hanbury, Bromsgrove B60 4BU. Telephone: 01527 821272. Off B4090 3 miles (5 km) east of Droitwich.
Open: Tuesdays to Sundays. Closed Mondays.
Skilfully restored farm buildings occupying three sides of a yard provide space for a range of attractions. There is a wide variety of craft shops and workshops with a covered walkway, an excellent restaurant and bar lounge looking out on landscaped duck ponds and a large room where craft courses and demonstrations are held throughout the year.

Malvern Hills Animal and Bird Garden (OS 150: SO 802410). 6 miles (10 km) south-east of Great Malvern on B4208. Telephone: 01684 310016.
Open: daily.
Monkeys, gibbons, wallabies and rare breeds of wildfowl are among the wide variety of animals at this centre, which also includes a snake house, pets' corner and picnic area.

Severn Valley Railway, The Railway Station, Bewdley DY12 1BG. Telephone: 01299 403816.
Trains run daily from May to September, and

Dunstall Castle Folly.

during school holidays and at weekends throughout the rest of the year; numerous special events at weekends throughout the year and Santa specials before Christmas.
Generally regarded as Britain's premier steam railway, the line runs from Kidderminster to Bewdley and then follows the valley of the river Severn upstream to Bridgnorth in Shropshire, a total distance of 16½ miles (26 km).
At Kidderminster the SVR station is beside the British Rail station. Facilities include the King and Castle real-ale bar with refreshments, and a gift shop. Kidderminster Railway Museum (page 87) is adjacent to the SVR station.
Bewdley station has a souvenir shop, a restaurant and an excellent model railway called 'Wribbenhall Junction'. Both Kidderminster and Bewdley have workshops for rolling stock repairs: the locomotives are housed and serviced at Bridgnorth.
The line enters the Severn Valley west of Bewdley and passes through delightful scenery where the Wyre Forest comes down to the banks of the Severn. There is an attractive station at Upper Arley, a former winner of the

Britain's Best Preserved Station competition. The line then continues upriver into Shropshire.

Timetables and information leaflets are widely available from tourist information centres (page 110) or from the SVR.

Twyford Country Centre, Evesham WR11 4TP. Telephone: 01386 442278 or 446108. 1 mile (2 km) north of Evesham at the south end of the bypass (A46).
Open: daily.

This large site between the river Avon and the new A46 comprises a garden centre, craft centre and wildlife and falconry centre. Facilities include a large café and a children's play area. There is river and lake fishing.

West Midland Safari and Leisure Park, Spring Grove, Bewdley DY12 1LF. Telephone: 01299 402114.
Open: daily, late March to end of October.

Here African lions roam a 5 acre (2 hectare) enclosure, through which one can drive, and the Safari Park also includes a hippopotamus lake, reptiles, sealions, pets' corner and numerous other animal reserves. The Leisure Park provides a range of rides from sedate traditional roundabouts to roller-coasters.

The estate began with Samuel Skey (1726-1800), who rose from being a grocer's apprentice in Bewdley to amass a fortune through the manufacture of dyestuffs from sulphuric acid. Having purchased the land, he built Spring Grove House and employed 'Capability' Brown to design the surrounding landscape, completed in 1780.

John Constable, who married Mary Bicknell, a relative of Samuel Skey, was a frequent visitor between 1811 and 1835. Sketches of the estate and the river Severn which he made during this time still exist. After many changes of ownership, the Safari Park was opened in 1973.

The memorial stone to Stanley Baldwin opposite his home, Astley Hall.

10
Famous people

Stanley Baldwin (1867-1947)

Three times prime minister in the inter-war period, Baldwin's popularity and political acumen contributed substantially towards maintaining stability through three major crises: the General Strike, the Depression and the Abdication of Edward VIII. Subsequently, he tended to be blamed for failure to rearm in the face of German militarism in the 1930s.

Baldwin was born at Bewdley: the house at the junction of High Street and Lax Lane is marked with a plaque. His father, Alfred, owned an iron foundry at Wilden, near Stourport. His mother, whose maiden name was Macdonald, had three notable sisters. One married Sir Edward Poynter, President of the Royal Academy; a second was the mother of Rudyard Kipling; the third, Georgiana, married Sir Edward Burne-Jones. It was this family connection which occasioned the remarkable series of windows in Wilden church (page 70).

After retiring from political life, Baldwin returned to his native county. As first Earl Baldwin of Bewdley, he lived at Astley Hall, 3 miles (5 km) south of Stourport-on-Severn. Here he spent his last few years, increasingly crippled by arthritis, and frequently worshipping at nearby Astley church (page 55). There is a large roadside memorial stone on the B4196 opposite the gateway to Astley Hall (OS 138: SO 800674). There is also a memorial stone near the west porch of Worcester Cathedral, where Baldwin's ashes were taken.

John Corbett (1817-1901)

Known universally as the Salt King, Corbett was a typical Victorian entrepreneur and philanthropist. Originally from Brierley Hill, West Midlands, where he worked in the family boatbuilding business, he came to the rescue of the ailing salt industry at Droitwich, introducing new methods of brine extraction and processing. He built new works alongside the Worcester & Birmingham Canal at Stoke Prior, 4 miles (6 km) north-east of Droitwich. They became the largest salt works in Europe. He improved the traditionally dreadful working conditions and lifestyle of the salt workers.

In Paris on business in 1855, Corbett met the attractive Anna O'Meara, whom he married the next year. In the 1860s he developed political ambitions but was unsuccessful in an attempt to unseat the local Conservative, John Pakington of nearby Westwood Park. Corbett commissioned a French architect to build a magnificent château-style house, completed in 1875, just north of Droitwich, and there he lived for the rest of his life. Today it is the Château Impney Hotel.

In the 1874 general election Corbett was successful but his life became beset with difficulties, commercial and domestic. There were labour disputes at Stoke Works and his wife ended a stormy marriage by leaving in 1884. Corbett was resilient: he turned his attention to developing Droitwich as a spa resort and, as the century drew to a close, revived the salt works, building fifty canal boats and four hundred railway wagons. By the time of his death in 1901 he owned, or had interests in, almost half of Droitwich. The Raven Hotel in the town centre is his principal monument, apart from Château Impney: a raven featured on his coat of arms.

Sir Edward Elgar (1857-1934)

Edward Elgar was born at Lower Broadheath near Worcester, in a cottage which is now a museum (page 88). His father and uncle were partners in a music shop, Elgar Brothers, in Worcester High Street. A notable customer was the Dowager Queen Adelaide, for whom Elgar's father tuned pianos at Witley Court (page 79).

From his earliest years Elgar was surrounded by people whose main interest was

The statue of Sir Edward Elgar, opposite the cathedral in Worcester.

EDWARD ELGAR

more widely known and in 1899 his *Enigma Variations* brought him widespread acclaim. This was followed in 1900 by the oratorio *The Dream of Gerontius*. Its first performance, in Birmingham, was somewhat disappointing but two performances in Germany in 1901 and 1902 did full justice to the work and Elgar's international reputation was enhanced.

The years from 1900 to his wife's death in 1920 were Elgar's most sustained period of creativity, during which he wrote *The Apostles* (1903), *The Kingdom* (1906), the *Pomp and Circumstance Marches*, his first and second symphonies (1908, 1911) and numerous others.

After his wife's death, Elgar wrote no further major works but remained an active composer and conductor until the final two or three years of his life. He was knighted in 1904 and made a baronet in 1931. He died in 1934 and was buried in his wife's grave at St Wulstan's church at Little Malvern (page 31).

An Elgar Trail leaflet is available from Worcester and Great Malvern tourist information centres (page 110). The walk in central Worcester (page 42), includes Elgar's statue and the *Dream of Gerontius* window in Worcester Cathedral.

music. He learnt the violin and often sat with his father in the organ loft at St George's Catholic church in Worcester, eventually succeeding him as organist in 1885-9. Elgar left school at fifteen and, after a short period of apprenticeship to Worcester solicitors, began to give violin lessons. He also joined a local orchestra and, like his father, played at the Three Choirs Festival.

He began conducting locally at the age of twenty-one, and this gave him his first experience as an arranger. In 1882 he visited Leipzig to hear the music and in 1883 his first orchestral composition to be heard outside his home district was performed in Birmingham.

In 1886 Caroline Roberts, daughter of General Sir Henry Gee Roberts, came to him as a pupil. They married in 1889 and lived in London for two years. Elgar's *Froissart* overture was performed at Worcester in 1890.

Encouraged by his wife, Elgar had now decided to devote most of his time to composing. During the 1890s he steadily became

Sir Rowland Hill (1795-1879)

Although best-known for his establishment of the universal penny post in 1840, Hill was a man of many parts. His family lived in Kidderminster, where his statue stands outside the town hall. Their business was ruined by the Napoleonic Wars and they started a school to recoup the family fortunes. Rowland Hill finished his own education at twelve and became a teacher in the school. Owing mainly to his involvement, the family debts were cleared by the time he was seventeen.

Hill subsequently achieved widespread recognition for his enlightened and democratic approach towards education. He built a boys' school, Hazelwood in Birmingham, for which he compiled a constitution and set of rules running to over a hundred pages. The boys themselves formed a school council responsible for administration and discipline. Corporal punishment was not used: offenders undertook community service to atone for misdemeanours.

Apart from a widespread interest in social reform, Hill was an inventor of some note. He developed an early aptitude for mechanics and became adept in the use of many tools. He became a competent astronomer and land surveyor. His rotatory printing press, developed around 1830, would have revolutionised newspaper printing but its adoption by newspaper publishers was prevented by the government department responsible for collecting the stamp duty on newspapers.

In 1833 Hill joined an association concerned with colonising South Australia and he was appointed secretary to the South Australian Commission in 1835. Around this time he sought to promote more widely his views on postal reform. It is said that his zeal in pursuing this arose from seeing his mother's consternation whenever the postman called. It was common practice for the receiver to pay postage: prepayment and standard charges were unknown. The service was expensive, often unreliable and far from universal.

A pamphlet on Post Office reform (1837) set out Hill's proposals for a prepaid postal service covering the whole of Britain for a standard charge. This met with considerable opposition from vested interests, including the Post Office itself. Hill persevered and eventually won sufficient support for the introduction of the universal penny post in 1840. He was subsequently appointed Secretary to the Post Office and undertook wide-ranging reforms. He is buried in Westminster Abbey.

A. E. Housman's statue in the High Street, Bromsgrove.

Alfred Edward Housman (1859-1936)

A. E. Housman spent his childhood and schooldays in his native town of Bromsgrove. One of seven children, he was the son of a solicitor, Edward Housman. In 1877 he went to Oxford to study classics. Although initially successful and an outstanding scholar, he failed to gain a degree because he insisted on pursuing his own preferred lines of study rather than those required by his tutors.

Back in Bromsgrove in 1881, Housman taught classical languages at Bromsgrove School, where he had formerly been a pupil. His father was now considerably incapacitated following a stroke aggravated by alcoholism. Housman quickly returned to Oxford for one term, achieved a pass degree and entered the Civil Service in 1882 at the Patent Office in London. From then on he visited his home town only occasionally.

During his time at the Patent Office Housman resumed his academic studies, con-

centrating on Latin poets. He published a succession of papers and the high quality of his work attracted such widespread attention that he was appointed professor of Latin at University College London in 1892. His first and best-known collection of poems, *A Shropshire Lad*, brought him public recognition far beyond the academic circles he moved in.

Housman was appointed to the Latin chair at Cambridge in 1911 and elected a fellow of Trinity College, where he remained for the rest of his life. He published a further collection, *Last Poems*, in 1922 and two posthumous volumes were published by his brother Laurence Housman in 1936 and 1937. His poem 'Bredon Hill' is the most widely known celebration of his native Worcestershire. Although his output of verse was relatively small, it contains some of the most perfect and familiar poems in the English language.

There is a statue of Housman in Bromsgrove High Street and a leaflet describing a pedestrian and a motor trail is available from Bromsgrove tourist information centre. His ashes are interred in the churchyard of St Lawrence, Ludlow, Shropshire.

Reverend G. A. Studdert Kennedy (1883-1929)

Nicknamed 'Woodbine Willie', Studdert Kennedy became a national hero and a legend in his own short lifetime as a result of his ministry in the trenches during the First World War. Well before he enlisted in the army, however, he was already secure in the affections of hundreds of poor people in Worcester.

Kennedy ministered in the Blockhouse, Worcester's poorest inner-city area, where he worked unremittingly to try to alleviate the worst effects of poverty. As a preacher he drew large congregations, both in his own church, St Paul's, and in the cathedral. In 1915 he obtained permission from his bishop to enlist and he became as widely known and well-loved in the trenches as he had been in Worcester. He carried two knapsacks, one full of New Testaments, the other crammed with packets of Woodbine cigarettes. Horrified by the carnage of battle, he made a point of being with his men where the danger was greatest, talking and preaching in the language of the trenches.

In 1919 Kennedy resumed parish duties for a time but, as a national hero, he was increasingly in demand throughout the country and he was appointed a chaplain to George V. In 1921 he resigned from St Paul's and spent the next eight years as a campaigner for numerous causes including the Industrial Christian Fellowship. He died in Liverpool in 1929, of pneumonia.

Worcester was silent and shuttered as the funeral proceeded from the cathedral to St John's churchyard. Today there is a memorial plaque in the cathedral and his grave with its tall cross is on the other side of the Severn in the suburb of St John's.

Charles William Dyson Perrins (1864-1958)

Usually known by his third Christian name, Dyson Perrins was grandson of William Perrins, founder of the Worcestershire sauce company. The family home was at Malvern. After graduating in law at Oxford, Dyson Perrins enlisted in the Highland Light Infantry in 1888. During his four-year period of service he met and married Catherine Gregory in St Giles Cathedral, Edinburgh. In 1892 he left the army, returned to Malvern and entered the family firm of Lea & Perrins.

While still a serving army officer, Perrins had been elected to the board of Royal Worcester Porcelain. During the 1890s he established himself as Worcester's leading businessman, the guiding figure behind the city's two major companies. The porcelain company slid into financial difficulties and Perrins lent £20,000 in 1898 to keep it afloat. This situation was to continue for thirty years until in 1929 Royal Worcester went into receivership. In 1934 Perrins acquired the whole company and from then on business gradually improved. His outstanding memorial is the Museum of Worcester Porcelain (page 91).

11
The story of Royal Worcester Porcelain

Worcester porcelain has made the city's name known throughout Britain and far beyond. This brief account provides some background information for a visit to the company museum (page 91) and a tour of the factory. The displays in the museum are arranged in chronological order, charting various phases in the company's development. More detailed and illustrated publications can be obtained from the museum shop.

The Georgian period (1751-1840)

Dr John Wall (1708-76) is regarded as the founding father of Worcester porcelain. He developed a successful career as a surgeon in Worcester and maintained a laboratory, where, with his partner William Davis, he perfected a recipe for soft-paste porcelain. A consortium of fifteen partners was formed and a company called Worcester Tonquin Manufactury was established in Warmstry House, near Worcester Cathedral. This site was convenient for the quays lining the river Severn, where fuel and raw materials from Cornwall arrived and finished goods were taken away. Early Worcester ware gained a reputation for not cracking when filled with boiling water. The earliest known surviving piece is the Wigornia creamboat (1751).

Dr Wall retired in 1774 and the factory continued under William Davis. Business expanded because tea and coffee drinking became popular in fashionable society, and in 1783 the factory was purchased by Thomas Flight, the company's London agent. The first royal visit, by George III and Queen Charlotte, came in 1788; they commissioned a breakfast service in oriental style called Blue Lily, subsequently renamed Royal Lily. This resulted in a royal warrant enabling the company to style itself 'Worcester Porcelain, China Manufacturers to His Majesty'.

Robert Chamberlain, the decoration supervisor, left to found a rival company at Diglis nearby in 1783. He established a good reputation, also receiving royal patronage and an order from Admiral Lord Nelson on his visit to receive the Freedom of Worcester in 1802, but Nelson died at Trafalgar in 1805, before the service was completed.

Meanwhile, Worcester Porcelain also continued to prosper. Royal orders included the Prince of Wales service (1807) in flamboyant Japanese style. Very high standards were maintained, with shells, flowers, landscapes and Shakespearean scenes being especially popular. A merger was, however, arranged with Chamberlain, and production was moved from Warmstry House to Diglis in 1840.

The Victorian period (1840-1905)

During the great expansion in consumer spending in the mid nineteenth century Worcester Porcelain added tiles, door furniture and buttons to their range of tableware and cabinet pieces. Factory modernisation in the 1850s allowed large-scale production of figures in a new material, Parian. It was combined with bone china and used to produce the Shakespeare Service shown at the Dublin Exhibition in 1853.

Worcester ware was now being displayed at major trade exhibitions throughout the world. Unique exhibition pieces were created to demonstrate the company's artistic and technical excellence. Highly gifted artists were given a thorough apprenticeship in the grammar of ornament, botany, biology and the study of Old Master paintings.

Royal Worcester was not the only reputable porcelain company manufacturing in Worcester. As the Victorian era drew to a close, two of the most successful were merged with Royal Worcester: Grainger & Company in 1889 and Hadley & Sons in 1905. Their factories were closed and production concentrated in the Diglis premises, thus strengthening Royal Worcester's already eminent position as the new century began.

The twentieth century

Traditional shapes and designs dominated the company's output in the early twentieth century, augmented by many individually commissioned crested services. Blush Ivory Ware was the most fashionable for ornaments and was produced in great quantities. A change of ownership came when C. W. Dyson Perrins, the Worcester sauce manufacturer, acquired the company and, under the influence of the Art Deco movement, a dramatic change of style emerged. Freelance modellers were engaged for the first time to produce popular figurines: pre-eminent among these was Doris Lindner (1896-1979). Limited editions were also introduced, pioneered by Dorothy Doughty

(1892-1962): her series of American birds stimulated new skills in the whole Worcester workforce.

In 1950 Sir Winston Churchill visited Worcester to receive the Freedom of the City and was presented with the Churchill Urn, painted by Harry Davies (1885-1970), the last indentured apprentice and regarded as one of the company's most accomplished painters. Davies was awarded the British Empire Medal for his services to the ceramic industry.

In 1976 Royal Worcester acquired Spode, but the two companies continue their individual traditions. At Worcester the specialities include fine bone china services, hard porcelain oven-to-table ware and superb limited edition figurines. The most popular of these in recent years has been Henry VIII on horseback by Kenneth Potts, introduced in 1990.

Hundreds of exhibits covering all periods of the company's history are on display at the Museum of Worcester Porcelain (page 91). This is the world's largest collection of the company's products.

12
Further reading

Reference books

Grundy, Michael. *Elgar's Beloved Country*. Worcester City Council.
Gwilliam, Bill. *Worcestershire's Hidden Past*. Halfshire, 1991.
Hurle, Pamela. *The Malverns*. Phillimore, 1992.
Jones, Ray. *Porcelain in Worcester*. Parkbarn, 1993.
Leatherbarrow, J.S. *Worcestershire*. Batsford, 1974.
Lloyd, David A. *History of Worcestershire*. Phillimore, 1993.
Lloyd, R.H. *Bredon Hill and Its Villages*. Self-published, available locally.
Meech, Julia. *Twenty Walks in Worcestershire*. SB Publications, 1992.
Pevsner, Nikolaus. *Worcestershire*. Penguin Buildings of England series, Penguin, 1992 edition.
Rolt, L.T.C. *Worcestershire*. Hale, 1949.
Salter, Mike. *Castles of Herefordshire and Worcestershire*. Folly Publications, 1989.
Salter, Mike. *Old Parish Churches of Worcestershire*. Folly Publications, 1989.
Taylor, Ina. *Victorian Sisters: The Remarkable Macdonald Family of Bewdley*. Weidenfeld & Nicholson, 1987.
Women's Institute, Worcester Federation. *The Worcestershire Village Book*. Countryside and NFWI, 1988.

Fiction

The novels of John Moore and the books of Fred Archer are widely available. Both evoke village life in the Bredon Hill and Vale of Evesham area in the mid to late twentieth century.

13
Tours for motorists

The tours described below encompass contrasting areas of Worcestershire and link many of the places and features described in this book. Each follows a circular route and can therefore be commenced at any convenient point and followed in either direction.

Bredon Hill (OS 150)

It is hard to imagine a more convenient tour: a string of delightful villages, linked by minor roads and encircling a hill which looks inviting from any side. These villages are on the spring line, located where streams emerge on the lower slopes of the hill. Bredon Hill is porous limestone, a Cotswold outlier, and therefore retains little surface water. In Saxon times, when settlements had to be self-supporting, each village would have had an area of the fertile lowland and a strip running up on to the hill to provide both arable and pasture land. Here timber-framed and stone buildings will be encountered, reflecting the contrasting landscape of hill and vale. The novels of John Moore and Fred Archer evoke life around Bredon. Footpaths lead up the hill from most villages.

Itinerary (distance approximately 19 miles or 30 km): Bredon, Kemerton, Overbury, Conderton, Beckford, Ashton under Hill, Elmley Castle, Little Comberton, Great Comberton, Bredon.

Elgar Country (OS 150)

First and foremost it was the magnificent Malvern Hills which inspired Sir Edward Elgar throughout his life. This tour concentrates on the hills and the contrasting areas either side of them. To the west are undulating lower hills and secret valleys, some just inside neighbouring Herefordshire. To the east is the broad flat lowland of the Severn valley. There is a longer, signposted Elgar route: a leaflet, available from Great Malvern and Worcester tourist information centres, provides more details about the locations mentioned.

Itinerary (distance approximately 30 miles or 50 km): Great Malvern; southwest up to Wyche Cutting (OS 150: SO 770430); south along Jubilee Drive to British Camp; Little Malvern Court; Little Malvern Priory; Malvern Wells (St Wulfstan's Roman Catholic church on A449 at OS 150: SO 773422 for Elgar's grave); A449 through Great Malvern to traffic lights at St John's, a western suburb of Worcester; A44 west to reach Elgar's Birthplace Museum at Lower Broadheath; back to A44, across it diagonally, and on to Rushwick; A4103 to Bransford roundabout and minor road to Leigh church and barn; minor road to Alfrick; back to Bransford; A4103 to Leigh Sinton; B4503 back to Great Malvern.

The Teme valley (OS 138)

In the chaotic conditions following the last glaciation great torrents of meltwater poured eastwards towards the Severn, creating the steep-sided valley now followed by the river Teme. It is a clearly defined valley with steep sides rising to the hilly country that comprises north-west Worcestershire. Hops are grown here: together with the neighbouring area of north-east Herefordshire, this is England's most important hop-growing area after Kent. There are orchards too, not the large regimented acres that are found in the Vale of Evesham but older plantings, often in secret little valleys and on hillsides. A particularly delightful feature, especially in springtime, is the number of damson trees lining the sides of many minor roads and lanes. This is Worcestershire's quiet corner, an area to savour at a leisurely pace.

Itinerary (distance approximately 30 miles or 50 km): Tenbury Wells; leave by B4204, in $^1/_2$ mile (1 km) forking left along a minor road past hopyards to Rochford, with a small Norman church behind a farm; continue all along this minor road to Stanford on Teme; right on B4203 to junction with B4204; left to Clifton upon Teme and Martley; B4197 north from Martley to A443 at Great Witley; detour right along A443 to Witley Court and church; back along A443, then fork right on B4202 for Abberley; return to A443, which follows the Teme valley back to Tenbury Wells.

The Vale of Evesham (OS 150)

Orchards and glasshouses are the prominent features that proclaim the Vale as one of Britain's premier horticultural regions. Through it meanders the delightful river Avon, busy with pleasure craft in the summer and a joy to walk beside at any time of the year. Most of the villages have expanded out of all proportion to their original size, but at the heart of each lie a village church and a street or two of delightful timber-framed or Cotswold-stone houses.

Itinerary (distance approximately 35 miles or 55 km): Evesham; A44 west to Wick and Pershore College of Horticulture; access to river Avon at Pershore Old Bridge; Pershore; B4083 to Wyre Piddle and detour to riverside village of Fladbury; minor roads to Church Lench; minor road to Harvington; A439 to Twyford Country Centre; Evesham bypass and B4035 to Bretforton; B4035 to Weston sub Edge and B4362 to Broadway; A44 to Broadway Tower Country Park; A44 back through Broadway to Evesham.

14
Tourist information centres

Most of the tourist information centres listed here are open all year and provide an accommodation booking service. Those marked with an asterisk (*) are open from Easter to October and provide an accommodation booking service. The centre marked with an obelisk (†) has limited facilities and no accommodation booking service; it is open usually from Easter to the end of October.

Bewdley: St George's Hall, Load Street, Bewdley DY12 2EQ. Telephone: 01299 404740.
Broadway*: 1 Cotswold Court, The Green, Broadway WR12 7AA. Telephone: 01386 852937.
Bromsgrove: Bromsgrove Museum, 26 Birmingham Road, Bromsgrove B61 0DD. Telephone: 01527 831809.
Droitwich: Droitwich Heritage Centre, St Richard's House, Victoria Square, Droitwich WR9 8DS. Telephone: 01905 774312.
Evesham: The Almonry, Abbey Gate, Evesham WR11 4BG. Telephone: 01386 446944.
Great Malvern: The Winter Gardens, Grange Road, Great Malvern WR14 3HB. Telephone: 01684 892289.
Kidderminster*: Severn Valley Railway Station, Comberton Hill, Kidderminster DY10 1QX. Telephone: 01562 829400.
Pershore: 19 High Street, Pershore WR10 1AA. Telephone: 01386 554262.
Redditch: Civic Square, Alcester Street, Redditch B98 8AH. Telephone: 01527 60806.
Tenbury Wells†: Teme Street, Tenbury Wells. Telephone: 01584 810136.
Upton upon Severn*: The Pepperpot, Church Street, Upton upon Severn WR8 0HT. Telephone: 01684 594200.
Worcester: The Guildhall, High Street, Worcester WR1 2EY. Telephone: 01905 723471 or 726311.

Index

Page numbers in italic refer to illustrations.